WHEN GOD CALLS YOU

WHEN GOD
CALLS YOU

Edward Deratany

THOMAS NELSON INC., PUBLISHERS

Nashville, Tennessee / New York, New York

Scripture quotations are from the *King James Version* of the Bible. Other biblical sources are from *The Amplified Old Testament* (two volumes), Zondervan Publishing House, 1962, 1964; *The Amplified New Testament*, © 1958 by The Lockman Foundation, La Habra, California; *The New American Standard Bible*, © 1971 by The Lockman Foundation, La Habra, California.

The material on Billy Graham appeared in *Billy Graham* by Stanley High. New York: McGraw-Hill Book Co., pp. 69-77. Used by permission.

The material on Peter Marshall is from *A Man Called Peter* by Catherine Marshall. Copyright © 1951 by Catherine Marshall. Used with permission of McGraw-Hill Book Co.

The material on Florence Nightingale is from *Florence Nightingale* by Cecil Woodham-Smith, as condensed in the August 1951 *Reader's Digest*. Copyright © 1951 by Cecil Woodham-Smith. Used with permission of McGraw-Hill Book Co.

The material on Tom Skinner is from *Black and Free* by Tom Skinner. Copyright © 1968 by Zondervan Publishing House and used by permission.

The material on Alan Redpath and Paul S. Rees is from *My Call to Preach*, edited by C. A. Joyce. London: Marshall, Morgan & Scott, 1968, pp. 105-110, 111-116. Used by permission.

Library of Congress Cataloging in Publication Data

Deratany, Edward.
  When God calls you.

  Includes bibliographical references.
  1. Vocation. I. Title.
BV4740.D45   248'.89422   76-6539
ISBN 0-8407-5601-1 pbk.

CONTENTS

PREFACE

Why and how this book was written are covered in Chapter 1. But it could not have been brought to this point of realization were it not for a myriad of persons. First, I am indebted to the thousands of young people who have crossed my path and influenced my life and thinking as much as I may have done for them. Their enthusiasm, openness, inquiring minds, and uninhibited affection have drawn from me a similar response. Their willingness to share their deepest confidences and their faith and trust in me have been a great challenge and an awesome responsibility. To them, humanly speaking, first and most of all is the credit for this book. I am lovingly grateful to my many young friends of days and years gone by.

Then I am grateful to other youth leaders who have shared their thoughts and experiences. I have been privileged to rub shoulders with them, not only within Salvation Army circles but from many other denominations; I have drawn many waters from their wells.

I have benefited from the writing of those who have transcribed the call of God. As much as possible, credit is given to them in footnotes, but I wish to acknowledge my personal indebtedness in this preface.

I am also indebted and most grateful to several friends and advisors who have read and forthrightly commented on on the manuscript. Their constructive and kind criticism has been of untold value. Specifically they are: Milton S. Agnew, Philip E. Collier, Joyce Davis, Merne A. Harris, Will Mayfield, David Riley, Glenn Ryan, Janet Shackleford, Minnie Belle Shennan, and my former secretary, Patricia Petrie.

Always and ever, I owe, more than words can express, much to my companion and sweetheart of nearly 35 years. Constantly, carefully, and cleverly she has influenced me in my experiences, efforts, and now in this production. I dare not say more lest I get carried away in an outburst of love and appreciation.

Finally, and above all others, I am grateful to the Holy Spirit, my Divine Guide and Teacher. In the final analysis, if this treatise is of any value or will be, it is because of His leading and blessing.

O the depth of the riches both of the wisdom and knowledge of God! how unsearchable are his judgments, and his ways past finding out!

For who hath known the mind of the Lord? or who hath been his counsellor?

Or who hath first given to him, and it shall be recompensed unto him again?

For of him, and through him, and to him, are all things: to whom be glory for ever. Amen.

Rom. 11:33–36

1
CLARIFYING
THE CONFUSION

"But, Major, how would I know if I'm called?" Barbara was a sharp, beautiful, wholesome teenager. Brought up in a Christian home, she was led early in life to make her decision for Christ. In the developing process another choice began to loom in her young life. What should she do, or be, in the future? Service to her Savior was inevitable. But *how?* And *where?* And *how much?* And *with what authority?*

Seeking counsel and guidance from whatever source she could find, she eventually shared her dilemma with the writer, her Youth Leader. In the midst of our conversation she wistfully, almost agonizingly, asked this question. Like many of her counterparts, she seemed sadly mixed up— groping for light and direction. As we shared some thoughts with her, she appeared to respond appreciably.

The light of God dawning in her heart was reflected in the peace that crept over her face. In response to her warmhearted thanks for the help she received, I facetiously responded with that cliché, "Some day I'm going to write a book on that!" I was not a little challenged when, in typical teenage enthusiasm, she exclaimed, "Oh! If you do, I'll buy a dozen of them." That response was never forgotten and challenged me to produce this printed labor of love.

Youth has its problems! This oft-stated phrase is one of the understatements of all generations. Since the young are long on idealism and short on experience, their problems are compounded as they hear many voices—loud and soft, convincing and contrary, wise and foolish, spiritual and unspiritual, enticing and repelling, base and lofty.

Nor is this bewildering dilemma the particular problem of the secular-minded. It invades the mystical realm of the spiritual life as well. This is especially true for most youth when one is seeking the will of God with reference to His divine plan for the future.

Soon after or simultaneous with the spiritual experience of being born into the family of God, the new convert is faced with the desire for the demand of service to God. For the older generation this generally means an adjustment to an already existing vocation or pattern of life. Not so for the young. With a whole lifetime ahead of them, the impact of their new experience presents a different set of challenges —and often frustrations.

QUESTIONS AND CONFUSION

In their idealism and attempt to find identification and meaningfulness for life, young Christians face, and themselves generate, a barrage of questions. To add to their dilemma, they are often confronted with the age-old challenge and urged to give their lives for "full-time service" and, almost in the same breath, cautioned to "be sure you are called." Innocently but unwisely, these statements often create more confusion than help to these sincere youthful seekers. Pity them when their minds become like a laundromat whirling about such questions as:

"What is full-time service?"

"When does it begin and where does it end?"

"How does it come?"

"What is a call?"

"How much less am I a Christian than someone else in 'full-time service'?"

"How does 'the call of God' come?"

"To what is 'the call'?"

"To whom does 'the call' come?"

"Are there different kinds of calls?—to different things?"

"How will I know when I am called?"

"How does it develop?"

"What should I expect—look for?"

"If I don't get 'called,' should I still go into 'full-time service,' or would it be wrong?"

B-A-I-K

Earnest and dedicated loved ones, friends, and counselors, in their desire to help and guide by their well-meaning admonitions to "be sure you are called before going into full-time service," have at times intensified the problems and created mental hurdles by citing such examples as Moses at the burning bush, Samuel hearing the dramatic voice of God in the temple, and Saul being struck down on the road to Damascus.

Although some may be helped with such counsel and illustrations, most others develop fuzzy notions, vagueness, and haziness. In their confusion and lack of understanding some young people use their disturbed condition to turn aside from the vocation of high purpose to which God would lead them. Still others remain in the deplorable condition of the youth who was seen bearing the letters scrawled on his jacket, "B-A-I-K." When asked what the initials meant, he explained, "Boy, am I konfused!" To the retort, "You don't spell 'confused' with a *k*, you spell it with a *c*!" he replied, "That's how confused I am."

Hence the "hang-ups" of Christian youth.

DARE I SPEAK?

A fully rounded experience with young people, which included fourteen years in the capacity of a pastor, followed by sixteen years as an Executive Youth Secretary, the first five on a state level and the last eleven with responsibility for the eleven midwestern states, brought the writer head-on with these problems of service to God inherent in the lives of youth. Interspersed with this work was an additional two years on the staff of the William Booth School for Officers' Training (the Salvation Army's West Point and counterpart for a seminary).

In several of the earlier appointments, it was my responsibility to encourage, recruit, and recommend young people for the ministry. Concurrent with the position of Territorial Youth Secretary, for ten years I held the position of Candidates Secretary (registrar) for the School for Officers' Training. This entailed processing the forms for the "cases" of all applicants, which included a form calling for personal testimony regarding "My call to officership." Additionally, I personally interviewed and counseled as many candidates as possible, which over the years easily numbered in the hundreds. Moreover, it was my privilege to meet literally thousands of young people in area, state, district, and local conferences; in camps and cloistered settings, unitedly and individually, with the responsibility of stimulating, encouraging, and advising them to heed the call of God for service.

This constitutes my humble claim to some right to make what I hope and pray, under the guidance of God the Holy Spirit, will be helpful and valid observations in this important field.

WHY BOTHER?

With growing sensitivity to these problems, there grew within me a strong desire to help resolve the issues and, hopefully, clear befogged minds of the illusory pictures that adults seem to create—either innocently or ignorantly. This was attempted in counseling and in public speaking sessions mentioned previously, as well as in seminars and forums convened for this purpose. Moreover, it became my practice to make mental notes from observations and interviews and to accumulate data from the aforementioned and very intimate papers on "My call to officership."

Much has been written about the Call of God, many tracts, magazine articles, and books with biographical references. The Bible is full of descriptive instances. Yet there remains much confusion in the hearts and minds of many young people and adults.

Having painfully witnessed these dilemmas in youth, I dedicate this book to the purpose of clarifying, especially in the mind of youth, what constitutes *The Call* (or the calls) for service and how each can identify that call for himself, individually and personally.

If the sparks of hope, ambition, and desire normal to youth are not kindled into some well-directed passion for God's service while the young people are still in their idealistic stage, they may easily fade into the ashes of a dead enthusiasm and destroy any hope that their possessors will ever measure up to the apex of service God wills for them. Such things as the choice of wrong companions, and undedicated life-mate, or a diversion from the spiritual to the material and the mundane can shipwreck their lives or at best steer them off course from the original plan of God. More of this later.

Additionally, it is the prayer and desire of the writer that this treatise may be a tool in the minds and hands of leaders and counselors who seek to lead youth out of the labyrinth of "konfusion." When a youth leader of many years of service was asked, "What is the greatest thrill of your work?" he replied, "Seeing a boy walking in the direction to which I have pointed him."

FORGIVE ME IF ...

If some of my young friends who read this ministry of words seem to detect a note of familiarity about some of the illustrations, it could be because I have borrowed a page from their own life histories. I pray none may take offense. In order not to violate confidences, some names and circumstances have been altered. Nonetheless, the illustrations are true-to-life and the people are real. These are mentioned in a desire to help those who have similar feelings, face similar questions and circumstances, and experience the same God who responds in similar ways. There is value in using these contemporary life experiences as supportive of the ancient and Biblical illustrations.

I am a product of my past. Hence, if the modern illustrations are Salvation Army–oriented, it is because it is what I have known most and best of all. Nonetheless, I have tried not to surfeit readers with an overbalance of Army-slanted examples. Hopefully, there will be enough of a general and universal application and appeal so that parents and leaders will be comfortable, even enthusiastic, in recommending this book to their youth and counselors.

2
CLARIFYING
THE CALL

The total will of God covers the total plan of God for the individual. The Call of God, whether for a single purpose or for many tasks, is the vehicle God uses to achieve His will. Therefore, the Call of God is always synonymous with the will of God, and the two, being interwoven, can never be isolated from each other. This is borne out by such Scriptures as Rom. 8:27–30(AB):

And He Who searches the hearts of men knows what is in the mind of the (Holy) Spirit—what His intent is— because the Spirit intercedes *and* pleads (before God) in behalf of the saints *according to and in harmony with God's will.*

We are assured *and* know that (God being a partner in their labor), all things work together and are (fitting into a plan) for good to those who love God and are called according to *(His)* design and purpose.

For those whom He foreknew—of whom He was aware (in the divine plan)—He also destined from the beginning (foreordaining them) to be molded into the image of His

Son (and share inwardly His likeness), that He might become the first-born among many brethren.

And those whom He thus foreordained *He also called:* and *those whom He called He also justified*—acquitted, made righteous, putting them into right standing with Himself. And those whom He justified He also glorified—raising them to a heavenly dignity and condition (state of being).*

MANY CALLED AND MANY CALLS

It would be extremely helpful toward a clear understanding of the Call of God to specific individuals, which is the theme of this book, if we were to recognize that there are several *types* of calls as well as many *methods* by which God calls. Though these two terms may overlap and appear identical, there is a subtle, and at times a strong, overt difference. A comprehension and appreciation of this multiplicity of types and methods will go a long way toward clearing the fog so prevalent in the minds of many individuals.

To begin with, the writer takes the position that there are, generally speaking, three types of calls common to *each* individual as he initially faces the challenge to become a born-again Christian. These are identified as:

1. The call to salvation
2. The call to sanctification
3. The call to service

The call to service may be subdivided into two types: (1) general, and what is commonly termed (2) full-time service.

At the outset, for our purposes and in support of our

* Italics added.

position (to be explained later) that this term "full-time service" is misused, we shall henceforth speak of it as "special service." If we seem to lapse into the error of referring to it by its commonly used term, it will be only as a quotation by those who use it—knowing that the sense of what they mean is a calling to "special service."

This "special service" comes about in answer to three other *types* of calls:

1. The mystical call
2. The circumstantial call
3. The organizational call

Because of varying theological backgrounds some readers may immediately question these classifications, particularly with regard to the "call to sanctification." Without apology to anyone, the purpose of this writing is to focus on "the call to service," be it of one type or another. There will be no effort made at theological debate. Hopefully, the heart of the message propounded here will have a universal interest and appeal.

Meanwhile, bear in mind that the terms and categories outlined here are not neatly defined entities into which each individual call will fit rigidly, totally, and exclusively. Far from it. If you were to ask a thousand different persons how God called them, you might get a thousand different answers. God never made us with a cookie cutter. Each of us is unique! And He treats us accordingly. Therefore, it is impossible to fit each call into any one particular mold. God speaks in different ways to different people.

In many separate revelations—each of which set forth a portion of the Truth—and in different ways God spoke of old to (our) forefathers in and by the prophets (Heb. 1:1) (AB).

In certain instances, some individual's experience may properly encompass two or more types of calls, simultaneously or progressively.

Our greater interest and concern has to do with (1) the general call to service, (2) the types of calls to "special service," and (3) the methods by which God calls. However, it is essential and would be most profitable for us to distinguish between and comprehend what we mean by the call (or calls) of God *universal* to *all* Christians. In fact, to bypass this would only contribute to the existing confusion about the entire subject. Therefore, as a springboard for what is to follow, we mention these briefly, emphasizing them as being the general will of God—for all mankind.

GOD'S CALL—TO SALVATION

God's *initial* call to man is to salvation. This clarion call is first heard in the records of the Old Testament:

> Turn to me, and be saved, all ends of the earth; For I am God, and there is no other (Isa. 45:22.) (NASB).
>
> Wait and listen, every one who is thirsty! *Come* to the waters; and he who has no money, come, buy and eat! Yes, *come,* buy priceless (spiritual) wine and milk without money and without price (simply for the self-surrender that accepts the blessing).
>
> Incline your ear (submit and consent to the Divine will), and *come* to Me; hear, *and your soul shall revive;* and I will make an everlasting covenant or league with you, even the sure mercies—kindness, good will and compassion—promised to David (Isa. 55:1, 3) (AB).*

Before Jesus called the disciples to be "fishers of men," He told them to "follow Me." Before Saul was anointed to serve

* Italics added.

God as king of Israel, the Scriptures commend him as "a choice young man and a goodly; and there was not among the children of Israel a goodlier person than he" (1 Sam. 9:2). Before the vessel could be used in temple worship, it had to be cleansed. The New Testament adds support to this general call to salvation—before service—more specifically "special service."

This is good and acceptable in the sight of God our Savior, who *desires all men to be saved* and to come to the knowledge of the truth. 1 Tim. 2:3, 4 (NASB).*

In reference to Rom. 1:6, John Murray comments:

The believers at Rome were examples of the fruit accruing from the promotion of the gospel—"among whom are ye also the called of Jesus Christ." The use of the word "called" in this connection is significant. Paul had previously drawn attention to the fact that it was *by divine call* that *he had been invested with the apostolic office* (vs. 1). Now we are advised that *it was by the same kind of action* that the believers at Rome were constituted the disciples of Christ. It is not probable that "called of Jesus Christ" indicates that Jesus Christ is conceived of as the author of the call. For uniformly God the Father is represented as the author (cf. 8:30, 11:29; 1 Cor. 1:9; 2 Tim. 1:9). They are the called of Jesus Christ in the sense of belonging to Christ inasmuch as they are called by the Father into the fellowship of His Son (1 Cor. 1:9).[1]

---

* Italics added.

1. Murray, John: *The Epistle to the Romans.* Edited by Charles Hodge. New York: Wm. B. Eerdmans Publishing Co., 1959, p. 14. Used by permission. Italics added.

GOD'S CALL—TO SANTIFICATION

There appears in the Scriptures another call subsequent to salvation, which is also a part of the will of God. This, however, in one form or another is directed to those members of the body of Christ, who in most of Paul's epistles are addressed as the saints.

> To the church (assembly) of God which is in Corinth, to those consecrated and purified and made holy in Christ Jesus, (who are) selected and *called to be saints* (God's people) together with all those who in any place call upon and give honor to the name of our Lord Jesus Christ, both their Lord and ours (1 Cor. 1:2) (AB).*

Paul capsules this call in 1 Thess. 4:3 in the words, "For this is the will of God, even your sanctification."

Dean Inge describes it most effectively, as follows:

> The mystic quest begins in every case with an inward call felt in *a moment of vision.* It produces a sense of dissatisfaction with ordinary experience, with those superficial aspects of life with which we are usually content. It awakens a great desire and longing to get nearer to the heart of things, and a hope that in doing so we may be rid of some of the discord and limitation and evil with which we are surrounded in this world.[2]

In his epistle to the Ephesians (4:1) Paul admonishes them "to walk (lead a life) worthy of the (divine) *calling* to which you have *been called*—with behavior that is a credit to the summons of God's service" (AB).* The calling

---

* Italics added.

2. Inge, William Ralph: *Personal Religion and the Life of Devotion.* Italics added.

to which he refers is set forth in Eph. 1:3, 4, the key to the entire epistle.

> Blessed be the God and Father of our Lord Jesus Christ, who has blessed us with every spiritual blessing in the heavenly places in Christ, just as He chose us in Him before the foundation of the world, that we should be holy and blameless before Him.

This calling is neither secular nor sacred. It is personal, experiential, and foundational to our position that there is *a call common to all believers,* which involves not only salvation but sanctification and service, even though we attempt to define these calls individually for the sake of clarity.

Depending on one's personal experiences and theological persuasion, there are some differences (which are very strong in some groups of believers) about what this experience is and how and when it takes place. Generally, where there is strong opinion among evangelical circles, it divides into the three schools of thought: Calvinism, Wesleyan-Arminianism, and Pentecostalism. And even within these three groups there are various differences.

Regardless of differences of opinion on this subject, Bible-believing Christians can and must agree on this one point— a holy God sent a perfect Christ to redeem sinful men, to bring them into fellowship with Himself. And, *He constantly calls us* to be holy, and *it is his will for us* that we be *holy,* which is a never-ending process. Alan Redpath tersely expressed it in these words, "You can make a convert in a moment of time, it takes a lifetime to manufacture a saint."

> (For it is He) Who delivered and saved us and *called us with a calling in itself holy and leading to holiness*—that is, *to a life of consecration, a vocation of holiness;* (He did it) not because of anything of merit that we have

done, but because of and to further His own purpose and
grace (unmerited favor) which was given us in Christ
Jesus before the world began—eternal ages ago (2 Tim.
1:9) (AB).*

Murray's further comments on Rom. 1:6, 7 add significance and support to this high calling:

"Called to be saints" or "called as Saints" places the
emphasis upon the effectual character of the divine action
by which believers became saints—it was by divine summons. They were effectually ushered into the status of
saints. "Beloved of God" describes them in terms of the
consecration which is the intent and effect of the effectual
call. Though it is without doubt the idea of being set
apart to God that is in the forefront in the word "saints,"
yet it is impossible to dissociate from the term the holiness of character which is the complement of such consecration. Believers are sanctified by the Spirit and, as
will appear in the teaching of this epistle, the most characteristic feature of a believer is that he is holy in heart
and manner of life.[3]

Agnew says of these same verses:

These people of Rome were both "called of Jesus Christ,"
and "called to be saints." What a call! What a challenge!
They were all invited to believe in Jesus Christ for the
salvation of their souls. They were also invited to become
holy persons by receiving the gift of the Holy Ghost.[4]

* Italics added.

3. Murray, *op. cit.* pp. 15, 16.

4. Agnew, Milton S.: *More than Conquerors.* New York: Salvation
   Army National Information Service, 1959, p. 14.

GOD'S CALL—TO SERVICE

As stated earlier, it is not the purpose of this writing to argue the fine points or facets of salvation and holiness. Let the theologians wrestle with and expound holiness and soteriology (that branch of theology which deals with salvation, partial or entire, through Jesus Christ). Our concern here is to attempt to clarify, for the minds of youth especially, what may constitute the *call for service*—what that call may entail and how young people can identify that call for themselves personally. Although the call for service must and may encompass the calls for salvation and sanctification (and they are in one degree or another prime requisites), this book will not seek to expound further on them. Nor will there be any attempt to stress the various *forms* of service such as preaching, teaching, missions, witnessing, and others, relevant and important as they may be. For our interests, suffice it to say that service, with salvation, and certainly as a part of a spirit-filled (sanctified) life, is essentially a part of the will of God. What that service is to be, how it is to be done, and when it is to be performed are yet other questions.

3

THE CALL
TO GENERAL SERVICE

The Call to General Service begins and is simultaneous with the Call of Salvation. In most instances, the Call to General Service precedes what we shall describe in a succeeding chapter as "special service."

In all of God's dealings with men He takes the initiative. He loved before we ever thought of loving. He gave before we could ever think of giving. And He calls before we could ever think of serving. Even though we can choose to serve (or otherwise), we are reminded in the words of Jesus.

Ye have not chosen Me but I have chosen you—I have appointed you, I nave planted you—that you might bear fruit and keep on bearing; that your fruit may be lasting (that it may remain, abide) (John 15:16) (AB).

Lest anyone experience a misconception that service or works are necessary to salvation, let it be emphatically stated that this is not the position of the author nor the intent of this interpretation.

It might be theologically argued that in its context this

verse was addressed to the original disciples and is irrelevant to our day. If *any* part of the teachings of Jesus to His twelve disciples is to be uniformly applied to *all* disciples that are to follow in *all* generations, then *all* of His teachings must equally apply. Furthermore, let it be repeated that those whom Jesus called were disciples first and apostles (special messengers) later. Consider the words of Jesus when He commissioned (thereby transferring *His* authority to) His disciples to become apostles, remembering the difference between a disciple as a follower and an apostle as one sent;

And Jesus came up and spoke to them, saying, "All authority has been given to Me in heaven and on earth. Go therefore and make disciples of all the nations, baptizing them in the name of the Father and the Son and the Holy Spirit" (Matt. 28:18, 19) (NASB).

We are disciples of Christ because we have been born again or regenerated and consequently have become a part of the family of God. With physical birth, subsequent growth and eventual labor are normal to life; so it is with the spiritual life. To employ another term common among Christians, we enter into the "priesthood of believers" *immediately upon salvation.* There was the time under the dispensation of the Old Testament and beginning with Aaron when only those of the tribe of Levi were allowed to be priests unto God. Now in the Christian era all believers become priests. Hence the salutation of John to the seven churches in Asia when he said,

Grace to you and peace, from Him who is and who is to come . . . and He has made us to be a kingdom, *priests* to His God and Father; to Him be the glory and the dominion forever and ever. Amen (Rev. 1:4–6) (NASB).*

* Italics added.

We should conclude from this that every regenerated Christian is called to be a priest and every seeking heart is a holy place where he can minister. How easy it would be to stay at home within the walls of a Sacred Sanctuary and bemoan the wickedness of the world. It is much harder to be in the front lines of service. But that is where God is calling us to be and *calling all who believe.*

THE WILL OF GOD

We have already established the Call to Salvation and the Call to Sanctification as prime phases of and essential to the will of God. Inherent in each of these is the Call to Service as *another facet* of *the will of God.*

There rests on each newborn Christian the obligation to use every opportunity and resource available to proclaim the gospel message. That individual's salvation experience automatically mobilizes him into action—if he obeys the will of God.

The story is told of a young woman, the mother of four children. After graduation from high school, she immediately married. Then came the children in rapid succession, providing her with a hectic pace. Taking stock of her life, she thought, "I never really pursued a formal education. In fact, when I take inventory of my life, about all I know how to do is change diapers and wipe runny noses. But the miracle of it is that I survived those years and it seemed like all of a sudden the kids were in school and for the first time in my life I had discretionary time."

Because of her Christian commitment, she felt an obligation to be a good steward of this new freedom to make decisions about how she might use this time. "I began to look around because I believe that in my relationship with Jesus Christ I, too, have a ministry. But what was I equipped to do? How could I serve?"

Her search for ministry brought her in contact with an

institution for the care of children who were essentially little more than human vegetables, "whose physical needs were such that . . . well, they really needed someone to change diapers and wipe runny noses." Then she related, "I have been going to the hospital while school is in session. . . . The interesting thing is that when I go to church, because some people have learned what I am doing, they say, 'You'll get a star on your crown for that!' and the most difficult thing I have to explain is that I'm really not trying to earn brownie points: what I am really doing is celebrating my salvation."

In his Epistle to the Ephesians, Paul admonishes servants to:

> . . . be obedient to those who are your physical masters, having respect for them and eager concern to please them, in singleness of motive and with all your heart, as (service) to Christ (Himself).
>
> Not in the way of eyeservice—as if they were watching you—and only to please men; but as servants (slaves) of Christ, *doing the will of God* heartily and with your whole soul;
>
> Rendering *service* readily with goodwill, as to the Lord and not to men (Eph. 6:5–7) (AB).*

Note that He equates physical service with witnessing and as service to Christ. All this is the will of God. To the entire church body at Ephesus, he admonished "Therefore . . . walk worthy of the calling wherewith you are called" (Eph. 4:1). Erdman comments:

> . . . This calling has been set forth in the chapters which precede. It was the *summons of the Holy Spirit* to *partake* of the grace of God, to enjoy a place in the Christian

---

* Italics added.

brotherhood, to reveal the virtues of Christ, to make known His gospel in the whole world, and to share His eternal glory.

"*Walk.*" It is a picture of one who is advancing step by step. *It reminds us of the common round and the daily task.* It assures us that every sphere of life gives one ample opportunity *to serve his Lord* and to walk worthily of his Christian calling.[1]

General William Booth, founder of The Salvation Army, in a challenge to seek lost souls, wrote a stirring article:

But who is to go? You! You who read this. Who else is there to go? . . . You are saved. You say your sins are forgiven, and that you belong to the family of God. You say the promises apply to you; why not the commands? Have one, and shirk the other? Never, never, never! They are united. Do not say you are a child and not a servant.

"You must go yourself." *This is a personal call* which comes down through the centuries to *you!* You cannot evade it and remain true to yourself and your God.

THE GREAT MISNOMER

On the basis of this proposition, this writer shares the strong conviction that the term "full-time service" is commonly misused and has an erroneous connotation and application. It has created an unscriptural dichotomy—a division of clergy and laymen. By implication the latter have been characterized as only part-time workers with partial responsibility, while the clergy and those in similar vocations were considered professionals in the service of God.

1. From *The Epistle of Paul to the Ephesians* by Charles R. Erdman. Copyright 1931 by Charles Erdman. Published by The Westminister Press. Used by permission.

How absolutely wrong! This misnomer might properly be labeled a trick and a tool of Satan aimed at lulling many to something far less than a full sense of responsibility. To that individual who would shrink from the will of God, it affords a ready-made excuse for taking the attitude, "I have less responsibility for evangelism and the winning of souls than those who are 'called to full-time service.' " Certainly, it has spawned fuzzy notions about the ministry and personal responsibility, and it affords great comfort to "spiritual draft-dodgers."

Futhermore, it does great discredit to the great host of faithful "laymen" who witness and give constant service, not only at their secular vocation but at home and during hours they might seek their own indulgences, yet choose rather to fulfill their calling to serve by teaching, visiting, and multitudinous other tasks, small and great! Literally, some more truly render *full-time* service than a portion of those who are labeled as professionals in so-called full-time service.

Just when and how this term originated is not quite clear. It is certainly not a biblical term. In the spirit of the entire economy of God, whether learned from the teachings of Christ or later from Paul and other sacred writers, it is never intended that there should be a caste system in the service of God.

Hans Küng, Dean of the Catholic Theological Faculty of Tübingen, states that the Greek word for layman *(laikos),* whether in the Gentile sense of one who belongs to the "uneducated masses" or in the Jewish sense of one who is neither priest nor Levite, simply does not occur in the New Testament. Rather, all believers compose the people *(laos)* of God. He writes:

The word *laos* in the New Testament, as also in the Old Testament, indicates no distinction within the community as between priests ("clerics") and people ("laity"). It indicated rather the fellowship of all in a single community. . . . Not until the third century do we find any distinction between "clerics" and "layman."

Elton Trueblood, the Quaker theologian, has declared that if we follow the New Testament seriously, we will abolish the laity and think of all Christians as ministers.

Finally, E. K. Simpson, Scottish Presbyterian exegete of Trinity College, Oxford, commenting on Ephesians 4, says plainly, "In the theocracy of grace there is in fact no laity."

Of necessity, in any army there must be generals and other commanding officers. However, they are *all* part of the fighting force. God never delegates only those in command to do the fighting, nor does He maintain a standby army. He has no reserves and there is never a discharge from the ranks.

Paul challenged Timothy to:

Take (with me) your share of the hardships and suffering (which you are called to endure) as a good (first class) soldier of Christ Jesus.

No soldier when in service gets entangled in the enterprises of (civilian) life; his aim is to satisfy and please the one who enlisted him (2 Tim. 2:3, 4) (AB).

Although the intent and use of the term "full-time service" are relatively understandable and well-meaning, it is nonetheless confusing and detrimental and at times does serious damage to the greater cause of Christ.

The story is told of a group of residents in New England who grew concerned about the many boats that became incapacitated and floundered off their coast while caught in stormy waters. Moved by a spirit of charity, they banded themselves together to more effectively rescue those in trouble. Eventually they established a life-saving station where they kept their necessary equipment and at a given signal of distress rushed to the rescue. This brought them a great thrill and satisfaction. Moreover, it united them in a spirit of camaraderie that was a joy to behold. Reports of their feats of heroism became widespread, and in turn other communities caught the same spirit. They too established life-saving stations, and the rescues multiplied.

In the course of events, these different groups organized themselves into societies to study better methods and raise money for equipment and organizations. Eventually, as the organization grew, the members found they had less and less time for rescue efforts and decided to hire persons to be stationed at the life-saving stations. Gradually, with the lack of involvement, the interest began to wane and one after another the programs died out. In time, pathetically, there were many abandoned life-saving stations along the coast of New England.

This was the history and nature of the early churches. It is the history of every newly formed nucleus that eventually becomes a church or a denomination. The early converts within these groups commence aggressively and single-mindedly in the winning of souls. But gradually, as the organization develops, which is normal and natural, those who take the reins of leadership, while continuing to carry a burden for the winning of souls, eventually find themselves carrying the major responsibility. Except for a faithful few, the vast majority tend to be indifferent and without a sense of responsibility for the service that is expected of all of God's people.

The corollary to this is that the mushrooming, explosive growth of the kingdom of God within these groups becomes arrested. Instead of becoming an aggressive force for extending the kingdom of God, the members settle down to being more of a social fellowship.

What else can you expect? As we turn over the bulk of service to professionals, we diminish in enthusiasm and thereby decrease the number of laborers in the harvest field. The task is beyond the few who are still faithful, and the paid professionals are then called upon to spend too much of their time nurturing the spiritual neurotics in the fold, many of whom normally would be healthy if they exercised their spiritual muscles in the service to which God has called.

This degenerating factor is further illustrated by the unhappy legacy of a world-famous violinist. He left his instrument to his native city on condition it should never be played.

Delicate woods such as those used in violins have the peculiarity that as long as they are handled and used, they will wear but little and retain their tonal qualities. As soon as they are laid aside untouched, they begin to decay, even though the process may be long and imperceptible.

Now in a state of disintegration, doomed to become a heap of dust in a glass case, lies this magic instrument of the great violinist. It might have continued, to enchant listeners for scores of years. How typical of selfish people who failing in service to God have degenerated into an introverted existence of personal interest. The chords and harmonies devoted to the uplifting of others have become silent, mute, and decaying.

God does not tolerate neutralism, nor does He allow for any conscientious objectors. Jesus explicitly said, "He who is not with Me (definitely on My side), is against Me, and he who does not (definitely) gather with Me and for My side, scatters" (Matt. 12:30) (AB). To paraphrase these words, he that is not actively *with* me is actively *against* me.

Thus, if we are members of the family of God and are interested in doing His will, which involves active energy in the fulfillment of His plan for salvation through Jesus Christ by the action of the Holy Spirit, then we cannot avoid a term common within the Salvation Army, "saved to serve." In the words of the Negro spiritual, "You can't go to Heaven in a rocking chair, for the Lord don't want no lazy folks there." There remains only one choice for *all* of us if we would fulfill His will, "full-time service." This is an obligation resting on *all* Christians.

It was said of Luther that by his preaching he opened the doors of monasteries and convents and thereby liberated men and women for more useful service. Concomitantly, he broadened the concept of vocation, which had been limited for centuries. Joyfully and triumphantly Luther discovered in the light of Scripture that "even the milkmaid can milk cows to the glory of God." Every Christian, he claimed, is called the servant of Jesus Christ in his work and in his station. As a Christian, this is his true vocation.

It is unfortunate that the church of Jesus Christ, in its narrow concept of "full-time Christian service," has so polarized the body of Christ that it has created this erroneous connotation that only the clergy or those who are on the roster of the missionary society have service to God as their vocation.

A world-renowned writer and author made the following statement: "No one *who has not heard the call of God,* should ever attempt to follow the highest and most sacred task, that of soul-winning." This appeared in a weekly youth magazine intended to challenge the young "to heed the call of God to full-time service." How confusing and misleading! Certainly this is not what Paul had in mind when he appealed to the Christians in Ephesus (4:1 AB) to "walk (lead a life) worthy of the (divine) calling to which you have been called . . ." To this point an editorial in *Christianity Today* commented on this verse:

> He clearly was not limiting himself to the "clergy" or to the field roster of a missionary society when he besought the Christians of Ephesus to "walk worthy of the vocation wherewith ye are called."
>
> The Christian is not merely called into the fellowship of the Beloved, he is handed a set of orders for his life. This may involve work, as with Nehemiah; it may involve denunciation, as with Amos; it may involve any or all of the spiritual gifts as set forth in the New Testament; it

may involve martyrdom. Vocation invariably goes beyond God's call. It becomes also our response to God by way of witness to Jesus Christ in and through our environment—or, as it might be termed, through our function in the social order.

When we ask where one is to perform the service to God set forth as the Christian vocation, the only answer can be "everywhere." Yet in reality the average Christian has only a limited number of places in which he moves; his home, his church, the home of friends, occasional public gatherings, a few streets, one or two centers of leisure time activity, and his work. In all of these areas he can and should be witnessing to his Risen Lord. So far the greatest uncharted, unexplored region remains the place of work.

The call of God is not one that brooks an uncertain or halfhearted response. God makes no "deals." He deals with man only at the Cross. Every committed heart finds its true vocation at Calvary.[2]

Let it be stressed again that the idea of service (or works) has no bearing on bringing about out initial salvation. We might even add that service need not necessarily be activity. The greatest service anyone can do for God is merely to surrender totally and completely to His will and faithfully witness right where he is. John Milton faced this problem. When first experiencing blindness, he struggled over what he felt was the apparent loss of ability to physically serve God but resolved this in his memorable "Sonnet on His Blindness"

> When I consider how my light is spent,
> Ere half my days, in this dark world and wide,
> And that one talent which is death to hide
> Lodged with me useless

2. Editorial: "The Lost Sense of Vocation," Christianity Today, August 29, 1960, pp. 26-27. Copyright 1960, *Christianity Today*. Quoted by permission.

Tho' my soul more bent to serve therewith my Maker
Lest He returning chide.
Doth God exact day-labour, light denied?
I fondly asked . . .
Who best
Bear his mild yoke, they serve him best;
    his state
Is kingly; thousands at his bidding speed,
And post o'er land and ocean without rest;
They also serve who only stand and wait. *

COMMON—BUT HIGH AND HOLY

This call to *general* service must not be interpreted as commonplace or lowly. Far from it! The difference between this and what is described as "special service" is not in quality or responsibility. Nor is general service less important. The difference is only in the *type* of service or vocation we undertake.

When on the day of reckoning we are asked for an accounting, it will not be on the basis of the positions we held but on the character of our service, whether in the so-called secular field or in sacred pursuits.

Our inclination to segregate these types of vocations is made with artificial barriers. The bread-and-butter efforts can be as sacred as preaching the Word. The Bible shows that business and religion do mix. Our Saviour worked with His hands. Paul the Apostle formed a lasting friendship with the Corinthians, Priscilla and Aquila, by joining them in their business. Paul regarded it a privilege to earn his bread by daily secular toil so that he might not be burdensome to the church.

History, past and present, has produced other examples. Henry Parsons Crowell was the guiding light in four sizable

* Italics added.

enterprises: Quaker Oats Company, Perfection Stove Company, Wyoming Hereford Ranch, and Moody Bible Institute. He not only changed the breakfast habits of the world and was a captain of industry, but he was also a giant in spiritual witness and service. In every area he exhibited his sense of responsibility for the stewardship of time, talents, and treasures to his Saviour and God.

Such was the devotion and dedication of R. G. LeTourneau, the renowned inventor and industrialist, who spoke of God as his partner in all his ventures and gave the greater percentage of his earnings for the direct propagation of the Gospel.

No less in service are the majority of unsung "little people" who have obeyed "the call to general service" and used their talents, time, and treasure to their utmost capacity. Many of them will get front seats in heaven not because they were in the limelight or in "special service" but because they gave God "full-time service" in their own niche in God's harvest field.

"Special service" may claim the full time of people, but this doesn't mean they are any more in "full-time service" for God than is the one whose vocation is butcher, baker, or candlestick maker. For *each and every one* there can be the dignity of service to which God appoints.

The writer addressing the Hebrew Christians (3:1) spoke of them as "holy brethren, consecrated and set apart for God," and describes them as *"partakers* of a *heavenly calling."* This epistle was not to a select, segregated few. Nor was it simply to those in "special service." Erdman comments: "The 'heavenly calling' may imply a contrast between the earthly promises to the followers of Moses and the hopes of things above shared by the followers of Christ." [3] We could reasonably insert by *all* "the followers of Christ."

Aside from the normal obligation for service that is im-

3. Erdman, *op. cit.,* p. 43.

plicit in the Great Commission and comes simultaneously with the initial call to salvation and service, there is a natural corollary for the infant Christian to do service for Christ. We know that in several instances after He performed miracles Jesus instructed those who had been healed to "tell no man." Yet because of the joy and the thrill of what they experienced, they found it impossible to keep silence. The normal and natural reaction was to spread it abroad. Why Jesus imposed this restriction is not fully known, unless it is that He did not wish to call attention to Himself until after Calvary. The important point for our purposes is that the adoption into the family of God is such a great cause for rejoicing that it is impossible for anyone who knows that experience to keep it to himself. It is true that there are millions who will never make God's Hall of Fame or be listed in the Who's Who of Hebrews 11. Nevertheless, as Ockenga points out,

> *"This calling"* refers to the *sum of one's Christian experience.*
>
> Calling is the work of God's Holy Spirit whereby men are brought into a saving union with Christ. . . . This *internal* work of the Spirit is to be distinguished from the *external* call addressed in the Word to *all to whom that Word is made known.* In this sense, "many are called, but few are chosen." [4]

4. Ockenga, Harold: *Proclaiming the New Testament; The Epistle to the Thessalonians.* Copyright 1962 by Baker Book House and used by permission, p. 102.

4
SPECIAL SERVICE

Customs, habits, and traditions are hard to change. For this reason, there may be some readers who object to discarding the term "full-time service" as relating to those in the ministry, at home or on the mission field. Conversely, the writer suggests the term "special service" as more realistically descriptive of that type of service.

DEFINING THE DIFFERENCE

This is not to suggest that the *person* called to "special service" is necessarily superior. On the contrary, the person so called may be very ordinary. The major qualification he has may be only a willing spirit. Elisha was a simple farm boy walking behind a team of oxen when God called him. Here was no talented Saul of Tarsus or charismatic Stephen But neither was there any lack of obedience or sensitivity to God.

And what about the twelve disciples? Note that their true call to *special service* did not come with the initial call to discipleship. The Amplified New Testament indicates this very distinctly in Luke 6:13, "He (Jesus) summoned His disciples, and selected from them twelve, whom he named apostles *(special messengers)."* And again, in Acts 1:2, ". . . after He through the Holy Sprit had instructed and commanded the apostles *(special messengers)* who He had chosen." It was only after Pentecost that they rose to prominence and honor. But how ineffective and common they were before that—not only at the time Jesus called them but even during their three-year seminary training under His tutorship.

Make no mistake—God's call is not usually directed to an elite corps of bluebloods. Consider those greathearts in the Bible. What were they doing when God called them? Moses was tending sheep as an exile-refugee; Gideon, threshing wheat while in hiding from a common enemy; Samuel, a mere boy doing chores in the temple; Saul, hunting his father's lost animals; David, a mere shepherd-lad; Elisha, plowing in the field; Matthew, gathering taxes; James and John, mending nets; Peter, fishing. In more recent years, David Livingstone was a piecer in a cotton mill; John Newton, later the author of *Amazing Grace,* a dissolute sailor; William Booth, a pawnbroker's apprentice; Dwight Moody, a shoe salesman; Billy Sunday, a baseball player; Billy Graham, a not-too-academically inclined seminary student, when God called each to special service. And one could name other prophets who had humble beginnings.

The man chosen to perform "special service" may or may not be extraordinary. But the *task* is! General Carpenter's daughter expressed it beautifully when she wrote of her father, "He had no illusions about himself. He was an ordinary officer with an extraordinary purpose."

The distinction between minister and layman is one of function; the nature of the service given makes the difference, not the spiritual essence. There is no essential difference in quality (except as it resides in the completeness or consecration of the individual) between the service of the so-called layman and the service of the minister.

The difference then between "general service" and "special service" must remain only in the type of service or, more specifically, the type of vocation to which one is called. The basic element of service is essentially the same. The following real-life experience demonstrates these points:

> The "bombshell" dropped in a matter of seconds. God— the Ministry—me. It did not happen in some great gathering, nor in some lonely place of meditation, but, surprisingly, in a normal Morning Service—and, of all parts in the middle of the Notices [announcements]!
>
> . . . Although I was prepared to do anything for Christ, the possibility of that "anything" including the ministry never entered my head, *because in the back of my mind was the firm impression that the ministry was for special* people, and *I was just an ordinary person.*
>
> . . . as the announcement was made, two things happened to me. The first was my realizing for the first time that *God called ordinary men to the ministry* . . . an immediate consequence. My ear was no longer stopped to the call. I became aware of the call there and then. God—calling me—to the Ministry? I looked at the pewdesk—could I ever lead a Service? My heart quaked. What about the pulpit? My brow went cold. Yet, as we stood for the hymn, I knew that what had swept over me in those few moments was something I had to face.[1]

It must, however, be recognized that regardless of how diligent in evangelism the so-called layperson may be, a great part of his attention must be taken up with doing a good job at work. If he fails to be a good craftsman, or at least a con-

1. Joyce, C. A., editor: *My Call to the Ministry*. London: Marshall, Morgan & Scott, 1972. pp. 19-21. Used by permission.

scientious worker, he fails to be a good representative of Christ. *In this sense only,* though it may appear to be a contradiction of all arguments presented heretofore, it must be admitted that the use of the term "full-time service" (misapplied though it may be) is understandable in respect to the ministry and related services. Those in the ministry may seem to have more time to give to that which is directly related to the kingdom of God. However, the true child of God will consider the office desk, the kitchen sink, and the factory lathe as much a sanctuary in which to serve as the church edifice.

This reasoning in no way is meant to belittle the office or importance of the prophet or evangelist or other type of "special service." Although the person called to such service need not be extraordinary, the depth of his faith and obedience may qualify him for it. In fact, quite often it does. In the true humility of one marked by God, he never exults in the honor or position to which God raises him as a leader and a servant. Rather he considers it all a sacred trust to be administered out of love to God and to human beings. To receive the call to preach is to be entrusted with a treasure; the urge to preach is an appreciation of the value of that treasure; the worthwhileness of that preaching is achieved only as that treasure is delivered as it was first entrusted.

OPEN DOORS

We can turn to the history of the early church for an apt illustration. Until a crisis precipitated his distinction, Stephen was totally unknown. No member of the inner circle of the disciples was he! For all we know, he was not even a member of the one hundred twenty who met in the Upper Room. At least he did not rate a mention prior to this occasion. Nor was he ever considered, let alone as a winning candidate, for the position left empty by Judas. His total experience, however, presents a fascinating picture in the scheme of God's call to men. It is significant that from a mere nobody, he jumped into the limelight through no effort of his own, but only because there was need for "special service." And there he was—willing to step in and fill the gap even at the eventual cost of his own life. There may have been scores of persons who could have done the job, but he and six others were "called" and "chosen" for this *particular* work, which in modern parlance would have been dubbed "The Department of Social Services." Certainly not a spiritually glamorous task!

In further support of our earlier premise, he alone, as far as we know, attained great prominence. This is not to say that the other six were not equal to Stephen in dedication or service. Indubitably, they too met the qualifications of "men of good reputation, full of the Spirit and of wisdom." We must also conclude that it was their *joint* effort (along with Stephen's fullness of grace and power in performing great wonders and miracles) that enhanced the spreading of God's Word and the marvelous increase of disciples. It is not mere conjecture to conclude that these men (all seven of them) had already been doing good service—possibly excellent service—more specifically, "full-time service" for God. But God had a *special* need for these men to do a *special* task, even though it might be rated far inferior in importance to that of the apostles who were led to declare, "It is not desirable for us to neglect the word of God in order to serve table."

From this select group, only Stephen made God's Hall of Fame. But what a loss if the other six had failed to obey this call to "special service" or to measure up to the challenge it presented or if they had vied with each other for prominence or position!

CLOSED AND OPEN DOORS

In contrast to those incidents mentioned earlier and recorded in Acts 6, we think of Paul *before* the Macedonia experience. He was already in "special service." Moreover he was being fruitfully used by the Holy Spirit. Almost unbelievably, in passing through Phrygia and Galatia, he was "forbidden of the Holy Spirit to speak the Word in Asia" (Acts 16:6) (NASB). Humanly speaking, he might have argued with God about this prohibition—this closed door. His frustrations must have increased when he was forced to bypass Bithynia and Mysia. But the Holy Spirit had other plans—plans for "special service" in Macedonia. The same Paul, with the same message, but called to "special service," in another country and another continent. This was simply *a change of orders.*

What would have happened to Europe if Paul had persisted in his arguments and pursued his own plans and method of service—good, legitimate, and fruitful service at that?

Henry Gariepy was one of those young talented officers in the Salvation Army who had a very promising future. Gifted in many ways, he was also equally dedicated in his vocation as a minister of the gospel. Then something happened. As with Paul, God began to close some doors and to open others.

Well on his way along the success route, Gariepy was uncomfortably disturbed by the Holy Spirit urging him to offer himself for "special service" in the inner city of Cleveland, an unglamorous, undesirable, but greatly needed ministry. Certainly this field of labor was not considered a mark of success in the eyes of his peers. Quite the opposite, it would be looked upon as a *step down* the ladder.

The human equation in his soul began to rationalize, "Why tamper . . . why take a risk?" But the higher qualities in him made him square up to the truth. To let the impulse of the Holy Spirit die would also spell death to the nobler part of himself.

Thank God his response landed on the credit side of the ledger. The philosophy and testimony in his own words are exemplary:

There is an approval I must ever strive to attain but it does not correspond to the echelons of human hierarchical systems.

Thus I can be people-oriented in my work rather than career-oriented. . . . My calling and commitment are not to program. I am called to something holier than program. . . .

No, I am not called to promotion, or position, or program, or even to production. But I am called to people and problems, to serve in the love of Christ and with the dynamic of the Holy Spirit.[2]

As of this writing, Gariepy is still serving in the Cleveland Hough area. It is the opinion of this writer that should he never rise to high levels of position or rank, eternity will place him head and shoulders above many of his contemporaries who pursued and achieved these attainments.

Catherine Marshall describes similar dealings of God with her famous husband, Peter:

Then in 1936 came the call to Washington, D.C. Peter could not bear the thought of leaving Atlanta. Surely the time was not yet, there was still so much to be done. So, flattering though the offer was, he refused it. Eight months later the call came again. This time there was no mistaking the by-now familiar tap on the shoulder: his marching orders from his Chief said Washington.

Through subsequent years there were tempting offers from important churches in other cities. On occasions the guidance was not easy to get; there were times when he struggled and strained to hear God's voice. But looking back now, I know that he was guided aright. *When a man intensely desires to obey God's directions, somehow God manages to get through to that man.*

2. Gariepy, Henry: *The Officer.* New York: Salvation Army National Information Service, 1967.

Peter received propositions of other types that tested this matter of God's guidance. A famous New Orleans attorney . . . made Peter an astonishing offer. . . . Compared to the salary of any minister, it was a magnificent amount.

Peter was as flattered by this as anyone would have been. For a few days he flirted with the idea. But in this case, the answer was not difficult to hear. It was a clear, resounding "No, you know perfectly well that I called you to preach. You would never for one moment be really happy doing anything else."

The years sped by. On the morning of March 30, 1946, Peter suffered an unexpected and devastating heart attack. It looked as if it might well be the end of the road for him. But that was not God's plan. "I have a surprise for you," the message seemed to be. "Some of your most important work is still ahead." When on January 5, 1947, Peter was made chaplain of the United States Senate, it could scarcely have been more of a surprise.[3]

OPERATION UNKNOWN

For some individuals the call to "special service" is not always clearly defined. Like Paul, Peter Marshall, and others, there are those who only know the call of God by a series of open and closed doors, *over* and *over again*. Note at least one more instance (though there are others) in Paul's life.

He earnestly planned to take the gospel to Spain, only to find himself in a dungeon in Rome. Frustrating? Not really! Contrary to his own personal plans and knowledge, this was his terminal point. Yet, from this dungeon, God pro-

3. Marshall, Peter: *John Doe, Disciple; Sermons for the Young in Spirit.* Edited by Catherine Marshall. New York: McGraw-Hill Book Co., 1963, pp. 20-21. Copyright 1963 by Catherine Marshall. Used with permission of McGraw-Hill Book Co. Italics added.

vided a pulpit, which in itself was far greater than any man
has ever accomplished in a lifetime since. Aside from any
personal contacts, sermons preached, and results he
achieved, we need think only of his "prison" epistles, six in
all: Galatians, Ephesians, Philippians, Colossians, 2 Timothy, Philemon. Who can measure the influence that these
have had on the lives of innumerable souls throughout
the history of Christiandom?

Not so simple was the urge from God to Abraham who
was "called to go out . . . not knowing whither he went"
(Heb. 11:8). To what extent Abraham enjoyed a relationship with the true God in a land of idolatry and heathen-
dom we do not know. In the midst of this situation God had
in one way or another—how we do not know—communi-
cated to Abraham. He in turn responded with faith. We
can also expect that he *made known his faith* and *served*
God fully according to the light he had received in the
idolatrous country. Surely here was a field where the true
Jehovah needed to be preached and known.

But, again, God had *other plans*. We can properly sur-
mise that Abraham enjoyed all the comforts and security of
the greatest civilization of his day. He could ask for nothing
more. Yet God stirred him from this comfortable, familiar
setting—opened a door into the dark unknown—and set
him on his way. To his credit, Abraham responded in a
way that assured his place in God's Hall of Fame—and God
saw fit to speak of him with high regard as "my friend"
(Isa. 41:8).

(Urged on) by faith Abraham when he was called,
obeyed and went forth to a place which he was destined
to receive as an inheritance; and he went, although he
did not know or trouble his mind about where he was to
go.
(Prompted) by faith he dwelt as a temporary resident in
the land which was designated in the promise (of God,

though he was as a stranger) in a strange country, living in tents with Isaac and Jacob, fellow-heirs with him of the same promise (Heb. 11:8, 9) (AB).

AS WE SAID THUS FAR...

Here let us briefly recapitulate what has been said. God calls all men to salvation, to sanctification, and to service. These are universal calls—none is exempt—and He alone takes the initiative. It is part of His will for *all* mankind.

The response to these calls is according to the measure of our faith and obedience. The fruit and rewards for the service rendered are according to the degree of faithfulness and not ability or natural talent.

Above and beyond the service God expects in ordinary life, He also calls certain chosen ones for "special service." This may be located at home or abroad. His choice, even as for "general service," is not dependent on our charisma but on His plan and will. Though honor and prominence may come from obedience, it is not to this that He calls. In fact, sometimes, as in the case of Stephen, those rewards may come only after death, even ignominious martyrdom.

Now we will begin to consider the *how* of God's calls in the succeeding chapters.

5

GOD MOVES IN MYSTERIOUS WAYS

"O.K.! O.K.!" I can almost hear youth impatiently cry. "I dig all that about the call of God to salvation and sanctification and service. I even dig what you say about service being part of the general call. I understand from the call to salvation and sanctification that I have an obligation to serve God in whatever sphere I am in—at school, on the football field, in the locker room, the cafeteria, in my social life, at my part-time job, and all that—but what about the future?

"I get the urge that God wants me to do more for Him. I have an idea I'd like to be a minister, a youth worker, a missionary. If God wants me in a field of *special service,* then I ought to get ready. I've got to make plans *now* and prepare *now* for that special service. I'm ready to move. But then I get turned off when I hear older Christians and leaders rap about 'be sure you are called.' "

HANG UPS?

"I've never received a call. At least I don't think I have! How does it come? How do I know what God wants me to do? Does He want me in the field of my particular interest —or in some other field? Man, am I all mixed up!

"What's all this about the will of God? How do I know what God wants for *my* life—not in the area of moral standards (I know and I can learn that from the Bible) and not in the area of devotion (I know that too; it is what God expects of all Christians), but with regard to my vocation?

"Is it wrong for me to prefer medicine, or teaching, or law, or the business world? How much preparation should I make, or should I just wait for that 'call' from God? And if I wait—how long do I wait? And what do I wait for? Just what are you saying when you talk about this business of a 'call from God' and 'the will of God'? If God is so great, He ought to give us some signposts. But where are they? And how do you read them?"

Youth has questions—real questions! And youth must have answers—solid answers! To embark upon a field of service—without the confidence and assurance of the will of God and His promised presence is to court disaster and defeat at the hands of the enemy of the soul. And the problem is compounded when this field of service is the ministry, where more often than not the task is demanding, exasperating, and trying to the soul and mind as well as discouraging to the spirit, and where most rewards are at best intangible. *Only a call from God* can effectively overcome one's reluctance to enter a profession so demanding. *Only a call* constitutes the divine authorization so necessary to undertake a task so sacred. To undertake special service for God, one should, like Martin Luther, have the compulsive feeling, "So help me God, I can do no other." This same compelling urgency is sensed in Paul's utterance "Woe is unto me, if I preach not the gospel!" (1 Cor. 9:16). One also needs the undergirding and comforting assurance, "Surely, I will be with thee" (Judge. 6:16), which God gave to a skeptical and shaky Gideon.

A survey at Asbury Theological Seminary made by a class taking a course on "The Life and Work of the Minister" sought to determine "the call's relationship to the ministry."

Although the survey lacked a large cross-section of participants, it revealed similar and typical reactions. The survey reflected the following results:

1. The call came early in life. It was very definite.
2. The call gave definite authority to one's preaching.
3. The call to the ministry is much different than a call to another vocation.
4. The call has never grown dim but has intensified. (The one minister who admitted his call had grown dim said that the reason was because he had seen other ministers quit the ministry and go into professions with more lucrative benefits and yet *maintain a Christian witness.)*
5. *There is undoubtedly a correlation between men dropping out of the ministry* and their *not having a call.*

GOD'S METHODS?

The questions still remain. How? When? If it were possible to select one or two or even a small number of individuals and point to them as examples, as a blueprint of exactly how God calls individuals, the problem would be easily resolved. Unfortunately, the answer is not so simple. Although the stress on "you have to be called" is commonplace and not to be underestimated, *how* the call comes and to *whom* and *for what* is more complex. To understand and explain these is impossible—but only when an attempt is made to comprehend them as an established *pattern* or as a *universal call,* in reference to "special service."

"The call" comes in a multitude of approaches by the Holy Spirit, tailored to persons of varying ages, different temperaments, and in a variety of circumstances. If God were dramatic in all His calls, the decisions of youth would be simple. For reasons known only to the Divine, this is not His *only* way. Nonetheless, the Holy Spirit calls men and women today with the same definiteness as Jesus did 2000 years ago.

Since we are not all alike nor are our circumstances the same, the all-wise Father, understanding these diversities of nature in His children and settings, uses ways and circumstances suited to the individual. To the one with an emotional nature He employs the stirring of the emotions. To another who is cool and calculating in disposition, the call comes by the Spirit's appeal to his reason. After weighing the question, he comes to the same decision as the more emotional one. A tear may move the first; an idea that develops with time directs the second. Some of us "see it all at once," others are slow to recognize His will and His call.

His approach may be *direct* or *indirect*. The audible voice of God is unmistakable in His communication with some. Visions and dreams still appear to others, just as they came to Bible characters.

With many others He speaks through the words, songs, and the influences of His servants. He woos; He invites; He challenges; He directs; He nudges; He even forcefully pushes. He uses a testimony, a text in the Bible, a phrase in a book, a situation that suddenly becomes very real. (A minister, trying to fix a poster on the wall, said to a teenager, "Give me a hand with this." He did and *read some words* that he knew at once had a special unavoidable meaning for him.) Youth experiences many voices calling. But youth's highest calling is God's call to service—particularly to "special service."

Some unknown writer has penned the following, which has come to be a classic within The Salvation Army:

The Call

"God in divers manners spake unto the fathers." He still uses a diversity of ways in making His claims known to His people.

Many young Salvationists [or Christians] seem to be wait-

ing for some spiritual earthquake to take place within
them, which they can interpret as a "call." But God comes
in the most natural ways to His children. The "divers
manners" spoken of in the text include the following:

To Samuel—the Temple boy—He came in the quietness
of the night when "the lamp was burning dim before
the sacred ark," and He just said "Samuel." So natural
was this Divine approach that Samuel thought it was Eli
who called him.

To Moses . . . for forty years amongst the magicians of
Pharoah's palace, God came with what looked like a
work of magic—a burning bush that was not consumed—
and Moses said; "I will turn aside and see this strange
sight," and God spoke to him out of the bush.

To Saul of Tarsus, "breathing out threatenings and
slaughter" racing along the Damascus Road in his work
of persecution, God had to come with more drastic mea-
sures.

The calling of his name, or even the magic of the burning
bush, would not have attracted him. God had to strike
him with physical blindness to give him a tangible illustration of the darkness of his soul. Then when [he was]
groveling in the dust, his name was spoken, and how
natural was the progress of his call. "Who art Thou,
Lord?" and "What wilt Thou have me to do?"

Henrietta Mears, who during her lifetime had a special
knack for influencing college-age youth (and others) and
exhibited deep spiritual insights, had this to say about one
particular field of "special service":

> What constitutes a missionary call? How
> does God call men today?
> The angel of Jehovah generally comes
> (Judges 6:11, 12) when you are busy.
> Saul was out hunting the livestock.

> David was tending sheep.
> Disciples were fishing.
> Luther was a busy pastor.
> Washington was a farmer-surveyor.
> Lincoln was a country lawyer.
> Frances Willard was a schoolteacher.
> Moody was a shoe salesman.
> Carey was a cobbler.
> You say, "Those men outside the Bible
> never saw an angel"? How do you know
> they didn't? God speaks to men in many
> different ways and surprises us as much as
> He surprised this young Hebrew farmer, Gideon.[1]

NO STEREOTYPES

Let us settle it once and for all—there are no set patterns that God uses to call men to special service, just as there are no set methods by which God calls men to salvation, sanctification, and general service. God sees us as unique individuals ("Are not even the hairs of your head numbered?") and deals with each individual uniquely. Consider the twelve disciples who are held up as Exhibit A. Note the variety of calls: some were direct; other disciples were brought to Jesus indirectly (Phillip brought Nathanael; Andrew brought Peter); and with the rest, including Judas, it is not even known how they came into this select group.

These different approaches by God are as common in modern times as they were with the disciples.

David Livingstone as a lad of sixteen was reading the story of Gutzloff, a missionary to China whose faith had conquered

1. Reprinted from Four Hundred Thirty-one Quotes from the Notes of Henrietta C. Mears (A Regal Book). By permission of Gospel Light Publications, Glendale, Ca. 91209. © Copyright 1970 by Gospel Light Publications, p. 32.

seemingly impossible difficulties. A grand dream that became an obsession captured him. He would be a medical missionary to China.

God moved in. An opium war blocked China. Then Livingstone had occasion to speak with Robert Moffat, a seasoned missionary in Africa. Moffat told the prospective missionary, "Do not choose an old station. Push on to the vast unoccupied and unknown district to the north. In that direction, on a clear morning, I have seen the smoke of a thousand villages. There no missionary has even been. There, sir, is your field."

The call of William Booth is familiar to Salvationists. His early ministry began with the Methodist New Connexion where his evangelistic fervor met with considerable and outstanding results. Feeling hampered by the dictums of organizational hierarchy to confine him to the pastorate, he resigned to conduct meetings throughout the country.

Through an apparently chance encounter with some Missioners, Booth accepted an invitation (was it a call?) to conduct a week's meetings in a tent erected on an unused burying ground in London's East End. Little did he dream in accepting this seemingly insignificant call that he was entering a door that opened to the sphere for which God for so long had been preparing him. So successful were his mission and messages to the unchurched mass that the workers pressed Booth to remain as their leader.

Returning to his home one night, the young evangelist said to his wife, "Kate, I have found my destiny. As I passed by the doors of the flaming gin palaces tonight, I seemed to hear a voice sounding in my ears, 'Where can you go and find such heathen as these, and where is there so great a need for your labors?' I felt as though I ought to stay and preach to these East End multitudes. And then and there in my soul I offered up myself and you and the children to this great work. Those people shall be our people . . ."

The Divine seal was set upon Booth's decision, and that

night, he said in later years, the Salvation Army was born.

The word calling has more than one meaning. It may include manifold voices. This multitude of voices may beckon toward a variety of objects. Hence, this author cannot fully endorse the oversimplification found in that beautiful but misguiding sentimental classic:

> And the selfsame voice is heard today,
> Calling to men in the *selfsame* way,
> As the fishermen heard by Galilee,
> "Leave your nets and follow me."*

Since the call to the ministry is very personal, we err when we try to force it into a stereotyped mold. God deals with each of us differently, and His will for each of us is different. Within the call of God there is room for individual variation, for the leadership of the Holy Spirit, and for each individual to work out with his God exactly what it is that God wants him to do. Just because someone doesn't fit into the same mold that God made for us doesn't give us grounds to determine that he isn't obeying the call of God.

Ronald J. Park's testimony effectively summarizes the theme of this chapter:

Who can define a call of God? We envy those who hear it as clearly as a human voice, or to whom it comes arrestingly as to Saul of Tarsus when his thoughts were set in the opposite direction. It left him no room for doubt or question. His course was determined. The glory of the Lord blinded him to all other considerations. But for most of us the drama is absent. God reckons on our understanding and guides our judgment as these are informed by a knowledge of His Holy Word. His call is as His breath upon our spirit, and our spirit feels, under-

---

* Italics added.

stands, knows and responds. It is the still, small voice of the Friend at hand, Whose mind is read, and counsels recognized, by an intuition wrought by the Holy Spirit, and does not require for confirmation the blinding flash of His Glory.[2]

INFLUENCES

Having settled the fact that there is no stereotyped call for everyone, we shall turn our attention to other facets of the call of God. But before we do, we should consider briefly the various influences that bear upon the call. This must of necessity allow a definite place for the human as well as the divine influence. God never discounts nor ignores the human element. Conversely, He uses it. At times He must counteract it.

Possibly the greatest factor, or at least high on the list, is the influence of early environment and training. This is valuable and vital to decisions made by children in early life when "religion is caught as well as taught." Properly impressed, such influences will not only lead them into a vital personal relationship with Christ but will remain with them throughout their mature years when they face the issues of vocation and service to God.

Little is known of the childhood and adolescence of Moses. What is recorded is that, after he was spared from infanticide, his mother was hired to nuture and train him. The impressions she made on him must have been effective. Although brought up in the secular courts of Pharaoh, he showed a tremendous empathy for and interest in his own people. His great mistake was that he sought to deliver his people by the force of his physical strength and personality. God had to send him to the desert wilderness to unlearn

2. Joyce, C. A., editor: *My Call to the Ministry*. London: Marshall, Morgan & Scott, 1968, pp. 79-80. Used by permission.

much of what he had acquired in the schools of Egypt. This certainly must have been a humbling process—and necessary.

When God saw that Moses was shorn of all pride and self-sufficiency and was ready to acknowledge his utter dependence upon God alone, He then appeared and called to him from a burning bush.

When John Newton was but five years of age, his mother, realizing her impending death, poured out her soul and strength in teaching and training her son in the ways of God. She died a year later. After a dissolute and exceedingly sinful life, Newton was caught in a frightful storm on the high seas that threatened a watery grave. During the experience he *remembered all his mother had taught him.* Following an act of sincere repentance and faith, he was miraculously spared and turned his footsteps toward service of God, which eventually led to active ministry. From his gifted pen we have such immortal songs as "Amazing Grace" and "In Evil Long I Took Delight."

Second only, and on occasion almost equal, to early childhood influences is the personal relationship between a minister or leader and a potential candidate. This is one of the most common factors in attracting young people into the ministry. Example again is the prime magnet. In their idealism, youth must see "the word made flesh," which radiates "the joy of the Lord" *in service* coupled with "the compassion of Christ" for souls.

Who can measure the example and influence of friends and associates? These with kindred and positive factors have much to offer as instruments through which God calls. A word in season from the right person has turned the face of many a youth toward the road where God would lead.

The response is typified in the testimony of one young candidate:

"I'd like to be like you some day," I remarked to the *minister.* "Oh," he said, "Do you mean that you'd like to be a minister?" I thought for a moment—then remarked, "Oh, I guess so."—It was only a child's admiration for good and a desire to compliment a minister which had sparked the conversation—but *it had planted a seed*—a seed which grew with my Christian experience. There was no thunder from heaven—no angel's tap—but *the call was there*—a nagging undescribable something that contradicted my every "No, I can't" with a "Yes, you must."

There followed nine years of balking, resisting, and arguing. But eventually the seed came to life. The candidate tells how it happened:

One night, a man quite possessed with alcohol stood before our open-air ring, and God seemed to say, "He's sick (spiritually), he needs help—this is your destiny." In my mind I debated—it's only a childish ambition. How do I know I'm called? I opened my Bible and Christ's words in bold red type declared "Follow Me and I will make you fishers of men." I closed it and opened again to another chapter, and again I saw—"Go ye into all the world and preach the gospel." A third time the Bible was closed and a third time opened—this time still another chapter —but the same words, "Follow Me and I will make you fishers of men." The words seemed to jump off the page at me. I could only close the Book and weep.

Still another type of influence is revealed by Luke, who is credited with the authorship of the book of Acts. He indicates a call to special service (in this instance by a change of orders), *by association* with Paul, who by some means or other unknown to us, had influenced him to share his work in "special service." Hear him as he writes the following words (note the change of pronoun from the singular, *as the writer,* to the plural, *as an actor* in this episode):

(There) a vision appeared to Paul in the night: a man

from Macedonia stood pleading with him and saying, Come over to Macedonia and help us!

And when *he* had seen the vision *we* at once endeavored to go on into Macedonia, confidently inferring that God had called us to proclaim the glad tidings (Gospel) to them (Acts 16:9, 10) (AB).*

Alas, how difficult it is to hear the voice of God when from some professing servants there is the clatter and din of criticism instead of a display of the joy of the Lord. The edge to God's call is likewise blunted when parents pursue affluency and prestige for themselves and their children rather than obedience to a life of dedication and sacrifice to His will. No wonder that some youth are "turned off" from the way and will of God as they witness false and double standards. No wonder God has such a difficult time reaching and calling them when such damaging influences have made their mark.

But, thank God, there are and always have been the positive influences of parents such as Sarah Wesley's, and Moses' and John Newton's mother.

NOT LEAST OF ALL

Above and beyond, as well as with, these human influences there is constantly *the work of the Holy Spirit* inherent in the call. As He moves with, and at times independent of, influences, He brings an inner pressure upon the will or a conviction that takes root in a man's mind, which drives him to action or instills a sense of a heavenly vocation that grows until the life is possessed by it.

Bramwell Booth in "Servants of All" (1899), after touching upon uses of different means to influence young people for the ministry, captions it all by saying:

---

* Italics added.

But it is not to any of these means, at any rate so far as we can tell, that we owe the large majority of the consecrated lives that are offered to us. It is rather to that direct and definite impulse, born, I believe, of the *Spirit of God,* which is usually described by those who recognize it as "the call to the work." There is, I admit, sometimes an illusion. There is sometimes, perhaps, an element of selfish ambition. There is sometimes, possibly, a mere impression, passing away more quickly even than when it came. But in the majority of cases that call is a very real, a very beautiful, a very powerful, occasionally a very terrible, visitation, exercising an extraordinary influence over the lives of those who receive it, and often bringing about results, both immediate and remote, which altogether astonish those to whom they are known.

G. Campbell Morgan endorses the same thought:

No man can go unless the Spirit call him. That is the high doctrine of the ministry; not even the Church, nor her theological halls. *He must be called of the Spirit.* Unless he hear that call sounding in his soul, ringing like a trumpet night and day, giving him no rest until he is compelled to say, "Woe is me if I preach not," then in God's name let him stay where he is, in his present calling. But if he hear the call, then let him remember that it is his business to go forward within the fellowship and under the guidance of the Church.

So much for the methods God employs in His calls. Certainly, we have not exhausted the subject—only scratched the surface. Also, we have only touched lightly upon the action and influence of the Holy Spirit in this operation. Truly His performance deserves a much fuller treatment, but we defer this to others in order to more fully pursue our stated objectives for this book.

6
THE MYSTICAL CALL

. . . *Suddenly a light from Heaven flashed around him;* and he fell to the ground and heard a voice saying to him . . . I am Jesus whom you are persecuting, but rise, and enter the city, and it shall be told you what you must do (Acts 9:3–6) (NASB).*

Who could mistake this exciting experience as the initial part of God's call? Certainly not Saul, later to be called Paul. Others might look dubiously at him, scratch their heads and wonder whether the noonday heat had affected him when he recounted the incident. But that would never matter to Paul. He was there! He saw and he heard! And that's all that counted.

How simple it would be and how easily resolved the problem of recognizing the call of God if all were as dramatic as Saul's and those of other Biblical luminaries who are so often used as illustrations of the call of God. Unfortunately, they are soon established as the fixed image in the minds of many (youth especially) as the norm for God's beckoning to "special service."

* Italics added.

However, to appreciate the full scope of God's plan and methods, we all must recognize that there are different types of calls.

In a sense, this may seem to be a contradiction of our earlier position that there is no set pattern in God's *methods*. However, to fully comprehend God's modus operandi in all this, we consider that there is a distinction between *methods* and *types*. At times, the two may be so interlaced that it is hard to distinguish one from the other. We cannot always neatly wrap each call into a package and slap a distinct label on it as we would on flour, salt, or sugar. Subtle as it may be, the difference is there.

It might be helpful to suggest that the *methods* deal with the *how* of the call; the *types* speak of the *what* or the distinctive features of the different calls. If somehow the latter can be completely comprehended, it will do much to more quickly lead youth out of the dark labyrinth of confusion where so many are wont to grope.

To explain our premise, let us first establish two simple guidelines. First our references to different types of manners in which God calls are directed only to "special service" and not to the call to "general service."

Secondly, for our purposes, we distinguish between *three different types* of calls to special service. This classification is not rigid and might well be altered by a different approach to this subject. In fact, a succeeding chapter will refer to a logical approach by another writer who deals with only *two* types of calls.

Finally, any one individual may experience more than one type of call, either simultaneously or at different intervals. Dick Rees illustrates this in his testimony,

> One summer's evening, the stillness of a Hertfordshire village was broken by a woman's shrill high-pitched voice, preaching in the open air. This was my first experience of Gospel preaching. I stopped and, still astride my bicycle, I listened. I understood nothing of what she

said. It was simply jargon to me but, riding away, I knew that one day I should have to do what that woman was doing.

Perhaps that was my call to the ministry. . . . A school-boy had called on me persistently for nine months and had persuaded me to go to the Crusader Class he attended. . . . *Probably that was my call;* yet it might have come when the Reverend Guy King challenged me with, "When are you coming to be my curate?" I laughed outright at his suggestion. How could anyone imagine me becoming a parson! Besides, my limited knowledge of clergy led me utterly to despise them. . . .

One day, visiting the restaurant which I invariably used when working in B . . . , I discovered to my great disgust that the place was full of parsons, apparently attending some conference in the town. What a bunch they were—dismal, gloomy, miserable, in many cases dishevelled, untidy and scruffy! "I am getting out of here quickly," I said to myself. I asked for my bill and paid it but, while I was walking from the cash desk to the door of the restaurant, *an inner voice said,* "You ought to be a parson." From that moment onwards, peace and joy left me and did not return until I had made an appointment with the Principal of the London College of Divinity and had committed myself to entering the college at the beginning of the following term.[1]

For more clarity, we believe it would be most helpful to distinguish between these three types of calls, as follows:

1. The Mystical Call
2. The Circumstantial Call
3. The Organizational Call

1. Joyce, C. A., editor: *My Call to the Ministry.* London: Marshall, Morgan & Scott, 1968, pp. 93-94. Italics added. Used by permission.

We shall concentrate on the first of these in this chapter; the others will be discussed in succeeding chapters.

THE DIRECT APPROACH

In many ways the mystical call is probably the simplest of the three types to describe, but the most difficult—if not impossible—to explain. This is so because this call comes about through a confrontation with God. The receiver not only has an inner awareness of the Holy Spirit, but there is a *direct* approach from God that involves the physical or the spiritual senses. To Moses, it was in a burning bush; to Isaiah, a vision in the temple; to Samuel, a still small voice; to Saul, a blinding light. As God made His appearance in these and other methods, He spoke directly and forcefully and each knew distinctly that it was God and each knew exactly what God expected of him. There comes an unmistakable knowledge of what the will of God is.

No wonder they answered! Who would dare disobey so distinct a call from God? Only *they* heard the voice of the Lord. Only *they* could obey.

Although these and other outstanding examples of this mystical type are evident throughout Scripture, nonetheless they are the least common. If one is to take into account all the priests and Levites who served in the temple and the hundreds of disciples who served in the early church, those who received a mystical type of call are vastly in the minority as far as the Biblical record is concerned. This is also true during succeeding years, and there is nothing in history to indicate otherwise.

Nevertheless, this secret, mystical approach is not altogether foreign to this day and age. Rare though it may be, there are still those who are privileged to have that direct, definite approach from God. Those honored in such a way are forever marked as unique servants of God. Such was the experience of Ray Gearing, a leader and missionary of many years service, now retired.

With regard to my call there really isn't any more to it than I mentioned in Chicago. In a Sunday night meeting I felt led to speak with a young man who at the time was keeping company with my sister. He had already gone to the penitent-form, and I was a little worried about the matter because I didn't think he would make my sister a very good husband. However, as I approached the penitent-form, *I very clearly heard a voice* telling me to let the fellow go and do a little praying for myself. I felt a definite call and I obeyed and made my covenant that night. There had been no call during the meeting. It was an evangelistic meeting and as far as I can remember nothing was said about consecration or obedience to a special call. However, I made my decision and went home that night and told my mother what I had done, and of course, she was very happy about it.

An equally dramatic call was that of George Harlott:

Returning home from the bakery one afternoon, I sat reading the local paper when my eyes caught the following notice standing out amongst the advertisements: Wanted, two young men as bakers, to sail round the world on a two-year trip. Apply on board the *Joseph Conrad,* now moored at the Cliff Quay, Ipswich.

Always looking for adventure, I was soon on the old "push-bike" cycling toward the Cliff Quay with visions of the wonderful adventure that awaited those who were fortunate to sail the high seas in this lovely three-masted sailing ship. By this time I could almost see us sailing down the River Orwell and feel the mighty roll of the ocean.

When approximately twenty yards from the ship, *I was suddenly halted in my approach* to the vessel, for *a voice distinctly said:* "If you want adventure, there is more than two years' adventure to be had in the service of God. Return and offer yourself for full-time service in the Salvation Army."

Within my heart I was assured that this was confirmation of a persistent calling I had endeavoured to stifle during the past two years and I felt compelled to answer this divine call, so, after making my way home, application was made to become a candidate for officership, and ultimately my star of acceptance was received on Easter Saturday.[2]

BUT NOT FOR ALL

Unfortunately, because this type of call is the simplest to describe and the most appealing to the imagination, it becomes the image that is so often pictured as the call of God. Herein lies the foundation for perplexity. Having no strange stirrings or fiery chariots, many an honest and willing youth has turned away from "special service" because there has not been this *dramatic* "call of God." The author recalls vividly how a layman, addressing a group of ministers, impassionately pleaded with them to be faithful to their task as shepherds and leaders. With tears in his eyes, he confessed that he had always envied their vocation but deferred from it because he "had never received the call." How tragic if this was because of an erroneous conception of the call!

Regrettably there are many other young people sincere, anxious, willing, *but uncertain.* Let none despair! Take comfort from the fact that even as in Bible days, the Moses' and the Sauls were in the minority. The youthful reader in the labyrinth of a similar experience should remember that God has other means of calling. But before considering these, hear the witness of Henri L. Becquet who pioneered with phenomenal blessing and success the work of the Salvation Army in the African Congo:

. . . My father . . . had dedicated me to God and did hope I would become an officer. Yet the choice had to be mine.

2. Harlott, George: *The War Cry.* Italics added.

I heard the first call to officership in a German prison camp in 1917, where I had been taken as a civilian prisoner, just after I completed my college studies.

I was still undecided. I was constantly pressed and pursued by the urgency of devoting my life to full service but *waited for a special sign which never did come.* One day at the close of a congress I surrendered, and deep peace flowed in my heart.*

Why God does not come to all in a dramatic fashion must ever remain a mystery this side of heaven. Maybe some could never recover from such trauma. Maybe for others human pride would swell and render them impotent for fruitful service. There may be still other reasons beyond our comprehension. In His divine wisdom God chooses other means, and in practical faith we must leave it at that and take comfort in the knowledge that there are other types of calls that relate to those of us not privileged to experience the dramatic.

That night . . . before going to bed I opened one of Oswald Chambers' books of daily thoughts on God's Word. The text for that day hit me between the eyes: "Whom shall I send, and who will go for us? Then said I, Here am I; send me." (Isa. 6:8). . . . Oswald Chambers wrote, *"Get out of your mind the idea of expecting God to come with compulsions and pleadings." . . . This is what I wanted God to do—to speak to me in some clear unmistakable way, perhaps to send some angelic messenger. For six months I had been conscious of the steady continuing conviction of the call of God in my heart. Now I saw that this was the call—there was no need for some dramatic confirmation.*[3]

* Italics added.

3. Joyce, *op cit.,* pp. 19-21. Italics added.

7

THE CIRCUMSTANTIAL CALL

"The need *is* the call!" For multitudinous laborers of God in "special service" this is the basic authority for their chosen vocation. Having seen the vision of a lost and perishing world, sheep wandering in the wilderness of sin without a shepherd, souls sinking in the pits of darkness, hopeless humanity imprisoned in a net of destitution and despair, and the Master Shepherd overworked for a lack of under-shepherds, they respond to the compelling force with the words:

> Precious souls are dying,
> Nerve me for the fight,
> Help me spread the glorious news,
> Liberty and light.*

One such servant of God who left the business world at the age of thirty-five to enter the ministry testified of his call as "a slowly growing conviction that *there was a need*. There was no emotional appeal in my life. I wondered if something was wrong. Ten years later," he added in the

* Song by Harry Davis.

same testimony, "I still can't stir up any strong emotion. But I have a sense of urgency that the job has to be done. It's fun being a minister."

There are those who would contend that "the need" is not sufficient authority for a call to special service. They would point to examples of persons who, facing the overwhelming and unexpected problems of the ministry or related vocations, turn from these pursuits, giving as a reason that they were "never really called."

THE HARVEST IS RIPE

In a later chapter we will discuss the matter of leaving spiritual vocations. No matter what reasons are given for forsaking the ministry, those who would minimize "the need" as a call would be hard pressed to rationalize the words of Jesus, "Do you not say, It is still four months until the harvest time comes? Look! I tell you, raise your eyes and observe the fields and see how they are already white for harvesting" (John 4:35 AB).

Farmers know that in the process of maturation wheat changes from an unripe green color to a golden yellow when ripe. But as it reaches the stage of overripeness and becomes nearly rotten, it fades from yellow to white.

From a brief experience of living on a farm in his boyhood days, the author recalls the excitement of the harvesting season. In that locale since the farms were comparatively small, farmers were dependent on hiring an owner of a harvest tractor who would contract with them to thresh their grain. By mutual arrangement, the farmers cooperatively gathered the previously ripened grain to the barns where the harvesting machine was situated. Meanwhile, in the kitchen of that particular farm, the wives and families of the men jubilantly prepared substantial and tempting victuals to nourish and refresh the laborers.

Occasionally, the operator of a harvest tractor would be

approached by a farmer with a request to come to his fields immediately. After consulting his schedule, he might reply, "I'm sorry, but I'm scheduled to go to Mr. King's, then to Mr. Scott's, then to Mr. Smith's, and I am not scheduled for your fields until next Friday." With great agitation the farmer might reply, "I know you have a schedule, but my wheat is getting white already." The anxiety of the farmer was caused by his wheat approaching the stage at which it would be beyond harvesting.

This same urgency is in our Lord's words "white for harvesting." The need of His day and the even greater urgency of our times, as "the day of His coming" approaches, impel us to *lift up our eyes unto the fields*. This must be the basis for "the call" to many laborers for fields of special service. Here is the example of Eva LeCornu who, with her cousin Stella, attended her first Salvation Army meeting in Adelaide, Australia.

Five hundred people crowded the hall, an old carriage factory, and Stella whispered, "We'll have to sit where we can."

Eva did not answer. Her eyes were riveted on the crowded platform where kneeling men and women—some in uniform and some not—were singing with earnestness and abandon:

He's the lily of the valley,

The bright and morning star,

He's the fairest of ten thousand to my soul.

"There's a seat," whispered Stella.

Still Eva did not answer. The upturned faces of the soldiers gripped her. People were going forward in response to an invitation, and presently, without ever having sat down, Eva was kneeling among them. "O God," she prayed, "let me realize the truth of those words as these people do, and I'll go anywhere and do anything for You." As she left the hall, a copy of *All the World* was pressed into her hand. Too wrought-up to sleep, Eva began to read a story of the slums written by Mildred Duff. Was it possible that people lived in such squalor and vice, thought Eva, and that girls no older than herself ministered fearlessly to their needs?

All at once she saw fields white unto harvest, and sensed a Voice saying, "Whom shall I send, and who will go for us?" Kneeling by her bed, Eva answered, "Here am I; send me." [1]

HURRY! HURRY! HURRY!

This sense of urgency is most graphically endorsed by the final great command of our Lord to "Go then and *make disciples* of all the nations" (Matt. 28:19) (AB). But you may say, "Is not this a command given to *each* believer? Is not this the basis for the call to general service?" True! We cannot minimize or disregard this. There are many in the ordinary, secular pursuits of life who witness to and serve their Lord either routinely or intensely. Gradually, for some, love for God matures, bringing about a greater understanding of His plan and will. This understanding may come about as a growing conviction, or the response to new or increased light, or the result of a total dedication to God, or it may be just a normal progression in the ordinary Christian life and walk with the Master.

Simultaneously this experience develops into an increased love for human beings and for the lost souls. Sometimes these visions come about during or after a traumatic experience. Sometimes God uses simple human agencies, but always under the aegis of the Holy Spirit. One young candidate testified simply: "You see a vision of the need—and you can't do anything else."

A youthful minister reflected:

1. *The War Cry.*

I heard no small voice, but my eyes saw the heart-breaking result of sin, and my ears heard the cries for "peace" from the masses of people on every hand.

God gave me life when the medical profession gave up hope. What less can I give Him than my life and what little smattering of ability I have. Today I still hear the cries of anguish, and I still see the great need. The Call continues to ring true in my heart.

Another, more seasoned, minister described it briefly, "God needed me, *I saw the need, felt the urge,* and *heard the call.* At seventeen, attending a Youth Rally, I settled the matter for good. God had a niche for me."

After over thirty-five years as a minister of the gospel, this writer can never recall when the point of decision to follow this call to special service ever came. Somewhere in the course of general service after being instrumental by the Holy Spirit in leading friends to Christ, there came the realization that this was a far more worthy, satisfying, and thrilling vocation than the original plans for the pursuit of a career in law. Gradually and unwittingly, I realized that the legal profession had lost its strong pull and attraction. There was no cataclysmic, sky-rending experience, not even a given moment or place that could be pinpointed. The call was silent but as effective as the process of leavening. The conviction of the leading and the call of God were and are as certain as that which came to Elijah or Paul.

God's methods of calling to a larger sphere of service are varied, and it is useless to wait for a call similar to the one some one else received.

The realization of the vast need is the call to some, and the strong desire to serve is the call to others. Many are called and in diverse ways, but only the individual to whom the Holy Spirit speaks knows whether or not he or she is called.

THE NIGHT COMETH

It is this growing and intense sense of urgency that impels many a dedicated person to rush to the harvest field, fully burdened with the reality that "the night cometh when no man can work." The challenge of a William Booth, "God and a sinning, suffering world call you to rise up and meet your opportunity. *Do it and do it with all your might,"* crowds the soul and furnishes a driving force. The only choice left is to reply affirmatively to the challenge to "leave all and follow me."

Dedication

Lord, can I dare sit idly by
And watch the millions Christless die;
Doing nothing to save the lost,
Afraid of what might be the cost;
Like Peter, warming at the fire—
Sheltering under the church's spire?

Dare I sit and waste the years,
Sharing Thy joys, but not Thy tears;
Unheeding Thy low, tender plea,
"Take up thy cross and follow Me";
While Thy footprints leave crimson stains
In city streets and country lanes,
As thou dost carry Thy cross anew,
Seeking the lost as I should do?

O Lord, forgive, I weep in shame,
I love Thee truly; in Thy name,
I turn my back upon the past
To wholly follow Thee at last! [2]

2. Atherton, William: *Dedication.*

The author vividly recalls the Ohio River flood of 1937. The disaster was great and the need even greater. All routine tasks of daily life were set aside. Business stopped, labor stopped, pleasure stopped, everything stopped while all efforts, strength, and resources were mobilized. There was a great need, and it had to be met and met *immediately!*

This is the basis for the intense cry of that passionate lover of souls, William Booth:

"Not called!" did you say? "Not heard the call," I think you should say.

Put your ear down to the Bible, and hear Him bid you to pull sinners out of the fire of sin.

Put your ear down to the burdened, agonized heart of humanity, and listen to its pitiful wail for help.

Go and stand by the gates of hell, and hear the damned entreat you to go to their father's house and bid their brothers and sisters and servants and master not to come there.

And then look the Christ in the face, whose mercy you have professed to have received, and whose words you have promised to obey, and tell Him whether you will join heart and soul and body and circumstances in the march to publish His mercy to the world.

Get up! Shake yourself! Act! Do something! Do it at once! Go on doing it! Do it with all your might! Spare no pains! Never stop anymore! Pray, talk, sing, give! Do anything you can—everything that will make the people know the truth about themselves and heaven and hell. God will help you. He helps those that help themselves, and especially when they are trying to help somebody else. He is pleased for you to help yourself to all the salvation He has to give you; but He is ten thousand times more pleased when you set to work to help other people.

I AM NEEDED

Bezaleel and his associate, Aholiab, are little known but interesting characters in the Old Testament. They are particularly significant to us at this juncture because they illustrate yet another need not commonly expressed.

Usually when we speak of "the need," the direction is toward the world—its plight and condition and its need of a Savior. Sometimes the need is for someone to proclaim the gospel and to labor in the harvest field. In a sense, these needs are objective. Out there somewhere there is a need. Out there somewhere *I* am needed. This calls for an intimate identification.

The need that Bezaleel and Aholiab typify is akin to these yet slightly different. For it involves something *that I have* which is needed, some particular talent, some skill, some expertise that lies within me that *God needs.*

Conversely, in the strictest interpretation, to use the words of Milton, "God hath no need of man's work or His own gifts." By the power of His might, as the Creator of all things, God could merely express "Let there be . . ." and it would be. Yet, in His design he has chosen to use the gifts He has given to men in the fulfillment of His will. No, in the absolute sense He doesn't need us or what we have, but—praise God—He uses both. This then constitutes a third type of need, equally important in the entire scheme of God's plan. It is a more subjective need—that which I possess, that which the Creator has endowed me with.

Such was the case with Bezaleel and Aholiab. On Mount Sinai God instructed Moses on the tabernacle, its furnishings and construction. How was poor Moses to achieve this plan in the midst of the desert and without the know-how? God anticipated Moses' problems and, referring to these two artisans, said, "I have *called by name* Bezaleel . . . and I, behold, I have given with him Aholiab" (Exod. 31:1, 6).

Their special service was not only to use their divinely bestowed talents but to teach others their skills and to oversee the entire project.

We are never told when or how their call came. The only inkling we find is later in Exodus, "And He (God) *hath put in his (Bezaleel's) heart* that he may teach, both he, and Aholiab . . . (Exod. 35:34). To this was added what God had previously said to Moses, "And I have filled him with the Spirit of God in wisdom, in understanding, in knowledge, and in all *kinds* of craftmanship" (Exod. 31:3) (NASB). A further thought might shed light on how the call came, "Then Moses called Bezaleel and Aholiab and every skillful person in whom the Lord had put skill, everyone *whose heart stirred him,* to come to the work to perform it" (Exod. 36:2) (NASB).

The end result was the absolute accomplishment of God's will, "And Moses examined all the work and behold, they had done it; just as the Lord had commanded, this they had done. So Moses blessed them" (Exod. 39:43) (NASB).

INDIRECT BUT DEFINITE

One final word about "the need" as a call. The mystical is direct; in contrast, the circumstantial in most instances is indirect. Remember, however, the two are not always separable. You may say, "I really want to give up my life to God, but I never heard any voice calling me." The great need of the world, its lost condition, or the opportunity to be the hands, or the feet, or the mouth of the Lord is a sufficient call for anyone who has the opportunity or talent to respond. The desire to serve God and the conviction of lost souls can take root in your heart and mind until it drives you to action—to special service.

The trumpet of God never gives an uncertain sound. We may never hear an audible voice in our ears, or see a burning bush, nor be blinded by light from heaven. Yet there can be an inner pressure on the will, which is just as compulsive. *That is the call!* But the word compulsive does not mean the same as coercive. The heart and mind must respond from within to pressures from without. Day breaks explosively in the tropics, gradually in the temperate zones. But there is no mistaking when it is day. The Holy Spirit stands at the door and calls; He does not knock it down.

William Carey said his call was an open Bible before an open map of the world, and he went to India.

Robert Morrison said, "Jesus, I give myself to thy service. My desire is to engage where laborers are most wanted." And he went to China.

James Gilmour, of Mongolia, decided the question of his field of labor by logic and common sense. "Is the kingdom a harvest field? Then I thought it reasonable to seek work where the need was greatest and the workers fewest," and he went to Asia.

Bishop Alfred R. Tucker, of Uganda, left a secluded artist's studio for the work of Christ. He had been painting the picture of a poor woman thinly clad and pressing a babe to her bosom, wandering homeless on a stormy night in the dark, deserted street. As the picture grew, the artist suddenly threw down his brush, exclaiming, "Instead of merely painting the lost, I will go out and save them," and he went to Africa.

> He wakes desires you may never forget,
>   He shows you stars you never saw before;
>   He makes you share with Him for evermore
> The burden of the world's divine regret.
> How wise you were to open not—and yet
>   How poor, if you should turn Him from the door.
>   Sidney Lysaght

8

THE ECCLESIASTICAL CALL

Tucked away in the fifth chapter of the Epistle to the Hebrews is a brief and easily overlooked statement, which has great significance to the subject of "the call of God." Described in that particular section of this letter is the pre-eminence to Christ's priesthood over Aaron's. This is done by comparison as well as contrast. In emphasizing the honor and importance of this office, the writer tersely makes the statement already alluded to:

And no man taketh this honor (of being high priest) but he that is *called of God as was Aaron* (Heb. 5:4) (AB).

CALLED! BUT HOW? AND FOR WHAT?

The succeeding verse comparatively points out that Christ, likewise, did not appropriate this office but was chosen or called by God.

So too Christ, the Messiah, did not exalt Himself to be made a high priest, but *was appointed* and exalted by

Him Who said to Him, You are My Son, today I have begotten you (Heb. 5:5) (AB).

Quite properly the writer to the Hebrews, under the guidance of the Holy Spirit, stresses the point that to do special service in the high and holy office of the priesthood, whether it is as a part of the human institution or in the spiritual realm (as Christ did), one *must be called,* which jointly includes *being chosen,* of God. However, for our particular consideration and enlightenment we raise the questions: *How?* and *For what?*

This writer, after making a thorough study of this important phase of Aaron's career, has repeatedly mentioned this phrase "called of God, as was Aaron" to Bible students and scholars alike, and then amusedly watched the look of bafflement that crept over their faces after posing the question, *"How* was Aaron called?"

Certainly, to the best of our knowledge, according to the sacred record, God never spoke directly to Aaron in regard to his call to special service. His initial orders to Aaron were "Go into the wilderness to meet Moses" (Exod. 4:28).

Moreover, there is no indication that Aaron ever *felt "the need"* for what became his lifetime occupation, which involved a sacred and special service for God.

But Aaron was *call and chosen,* if we are to believe the writer to the Hebrews and for that matter if we are to believe the entire Bible.

HUMAN INSTRUMENTALITY

But how? The answer is simple and must be recognized for what it is—another *type* of call.

After God had outlined to Moses the details of the tabernacle and the office of the High Priest, He in essence instructed Moses, "You *tell* Aaron on my behalf, 'I choose you and your lineage to be the High Priest. I need you and want you, hence I call you.' "

Two aspects of this event are significant. First, the call to Aaron came *indirectly from God—through Moses.* Secondly, it was the initial call of God for special service to an organization—to a church (as structured in the Old Testament).

Hence we have the term, "ecclesiastical call," or the "organizational call."

The fact that this call came through the instrument of a man did not minimize its importance. Aaron was altogether a man "called of God." He was God's choice and God's anointed, though Moses did the physical anointing. Thus, we have the foundation for a third and often overlooked type of call.

In a similar manner, though to an office of lesser degree, the Levites were chosen to serve in the tabernacle. Granted their service included only supportive and routine tasks, nonetheless, it was special service for which God called and chose them.

Quite correctly the story of Bezaleel and Aholiab recounted in the previous chapter could also be labeled as an "eccleciastical call" as well as a "circumstantial call." A similar modern illustration of the organizational call is related by Ivy Waterworth,

> It was a day like all other days . . . that alter and illuminate our times . . . and I was there! . . . The Editor-in-Chief stopped at my door to say: "The Commissioner wants to see you." . . . Then I heard the Commissioner say: "I have a letter from the National Commander to say that the Army needs an officer for an overseas territory."
>
> To say that I had ever heard a direct Call to the mission field would hardly be accurate. I have never felt a definite urge to foreign service. . . .
>
> The Divine Call did not come to me in any great and glorious assembly, with colors waving and band playing and soldiers marching. It came in the quiet of my own

home—as a still, small voice that I, alone, could hear. And with all its stillness, it broke my spirit so completely that I could do nothing but surrender.

When God called me, He did not hand me a rail ticket to Atlanta, nor a flight ticket to San Francisco. He simply said, "I need you!"

There was no promise of success, or advancement; no offer of rapid promotion that would skyrocket me to the top before my comrades. There was no guarantee that I should even have three square meals a day. But there was a *call* from God, and there was a *need* to be met.

That same *call* and that same *need* were present when the Commissioner called me to his office. That same *call* and that same *need* are present today.[1]

The first indication we ever have that God called Joshua, Moses' successor, to special service is recorded in Numbers: "And the Lord said unto Moses, Take thee Joshua the son of Nun, a man in whom is the spirit, and lay thine hand upon him . . . and give him a charge!" (Num. 27:18, 19).

It is again emphasized that it was through Moses, a human instrument as the mouthpiece of God, that He called Joshua to lead that great host of Israelites, God's chosen people. Once again, God's call came *indirectly, through a man to a man.*

Then Moses called to Joshua and said to him in the sight of all Israel, Be strong and courageous, for you shall go with this people into the land which the Lord has sworn to their fathers to give them, and you shall give it to them as an inheritance.

And the Lord is the one who goes ahead of you; He will be with you. He will not fail you or forsake you. Do not fear, or be dismayed (Deut. 31:7, 8) (NASB).

1. Waterworth, Ivy: *The Young Soldier.* New York: The Salvation Army National Information Service.

Only after Moses had died do we have any record that God ever spoke directly with Joshua (Josh. 1:1). The ecclesiastical call to special service had taken place long before that and was already a settled issue.

One of the earliest instances recorded in the Bible of an organizational call is found in Exodus. When Jethro, Moses' father-in-law, learned of God's deliverance of the children of Israel, he brought Moses' wife and two sons and visited with him. During the visit he noticed that Moses spent the entire day teaching, instructing, and judging the people as they brought their problems and sought to learn of God from him. The astute old man mildly reprimanded Moses with the words:

> The thing that you are doing is not good. You will surely wear out, both yourself and these people who are with you, for the task is too heavy for you; you cannot do it alone (Exod. 18:17, 18) (NASB).

Then, judiciously, he continued:

> Now listen to me: I shall give you counsel, and God be with you. You be the people's representative before God, and you bring the disputes to God,
>
> Then teach them the statutes and the law, and make known to them the way in which they are to walk, and the work they are to do.
>
> Furthermore, *you* shall select out of all the people able men who fear God, men of truth, those who hate dishonest gain; and you shall place these over them, as leaders of thousands, of hundreds, of fifties and of tens.
>
> And let them judge the people at all times; and let it be that every major dispute they will bring to you, but every minor dispute they themselves will judge. So it will be easier for you, and they will bear the burden with you.
>
> If you do this thing and God so commands you, then

you will be able to endure, and all these people also will go to their place in peace (Exod. 18:19–23) (NASB).

To the credit of Moses, he "hearkened to the voice of his father-in-law, and did all that he said." Can there be any better illustration of an organizational need coupled with an indirect call to special service for God—a call from God's man to God's men?

IT HAPPENED AGAIN

A counterpart to all this is found in a most significant event in the early history of the New Testament church. A crisis arose because of the fact that the physical needs of a disadvantaged segment of the church were being neglected. Apparently, in their zeal to proclaim the gospel and witness to the resurrection and power of Christ, the corporate body of Christ had overlooked this mundane necessity and duty. Rather than shrug it off as too unspiritual or unrelated to their responsibility and dignity as leaders of the church, the twelve disciples took the necessary steps to strengthen the work of their embryonic organization.

The process they followed, which eventuated in the choosing and calling of Stephen and the other six for special service, is most interesting and significant. Under the guidance of the Holy Spirit they instructed the "multitude of the disciples" to select the seven qualified men (an unprecedented democratic process) and they (the twelve) in turn appointed them (the seven) "to look after *this business* and duty" and "*after* prayer laid their hands on them" (Acts 6:3, 6) (AB). Again, there were no visions, no voice of God, not even the sense of an urgent need as far as the seven were personally concerned. Simply stated, there was an organizational need, and the anointed leaders of God, the apostles, called these qualified servants of God into special service. Note that before they issued their call, the congregation itself selected, chose, and called these seven men to special service for God.

Apparently the process was profitable and had the blessing of God, as evidenced by the subsequent results:

And the word of God kept on speaking; and the number of the disciples continued to increase greatly in Jerusalem, and a great many of the priests were becoming obedient to the faith (Acts 6:7) (NASB).

Dare anyone challenge this as the unqualified "call of God," indirect and human-channeled though it was? Dare anyone deny that this was for an institutional or organizational need?

In some circles it seems to be quite popular to rebel against and even ridicule the modern "institutional church" as irrelevant to the space age and cumbersome to the effective propagation of the Gospel. To deny that there are weaknesses in the organized church and that its administration by some leaders in office is more political than spiritual would be to speak with blindness. But equally so, to write off all churches and related organizations as archaic or fruitless is to deny many members their place in the body of Christ.

It is the nature of all movements, good or bad, eventually to organize, in order to maintain their purposes and develop their growth. In the beginning they tend to be provincial in concept and jealous of their own group. Initially, all or most workers in their own particular movement are imbued with an intense desire and drive to make Christ known as the result of their own personal experience with Christ and, simultaneously, the call to general service. To begin with, little or no attention is paid to formal training or education. Like the early New Testament church, the movement expands vigorously. Then, when problems arise as they always do and when there is an increase of people in the movement (remember the story of Stephen in Acts 6?), it becomes advisable and necessary to form some kind of an organization.

It is regrettable that as these organizations grow and mature they tend to lose some of their ideals, motivation, and drive unless they are perpetually renewed and rejuvenated.

But organizations we have and will always have, as long as God allows. And as long as they exist, ecclesiastical bodies have need of dedicated people who are "called of God" to maintain their work for the Lord. Like the Biblical examples given previously, that call must come from God, generally through one individual to another. Usually, the leaders see and feel the need for preachers, missionaries, teachers, administrators, Stephen-like relief workers, and priestlike cleaners of ashes from the sacrificial altars. In good scriptural tradition, not unlike the Master, they press the claims of Christ, and hence the call.

Often this type of service is the least glamorous; it lacks emotional appeal and excitement, and certainly is not colorful. Basically, however, in many ways it is most important and necessary. It is the oil that keeps the machinery moving smoothly. It allows those called to preach and teach to not "leave the word of God, and serve tables" (Acts 6:2) but to "give ourselves continually to prayer, and to the ministry of the word" (Acts 6:4).

ONE BODY—MANY PARTS

The word ecclesiastical comes from the Greek word *"ecclesia,"* which is interpreted to mean "assembly" and is the New Testament term for "church" or "congregation." The church is also spoken of as a body. This is supported by much Scripture, for example, in Paul's first epistle to the Corinthians,

For even as the body is one and *yet* has many members, and all the members of the body, though they are many, are *one body,* so also is Christ.

For by one Spirit we are all baptized into one body, whether Jews or Greeks, whether slaves or free, and we were all made to drink of one spirit.

For the body is not one member, but many.

If the foot should say, Because I am not a hand, I am not a part of the body, it is not for this reason any the less a part of the body.

And if the ear should say, Because I am not an eye, I am not a part of the body, it is not for this reason any the less a part of the body.

If the whole body were an eye, where would the hearing be? If the whole were hearing, where would the sense of smell be ?

But now God has placed the members, each one of them, in the body, just as He desired (1 Cor. 12:12–18) (NASB).

The apostle also says practically the same thing to the church at Rome. In listing the gifts of faculties, talents, and qualities he urges the use of these, each as part of the body (which must be well coordinated, or organized, to function properly) of Christ. Interestingly, with other coveted talents, Paul refers to ". . . (He whose gift is) *practical* service, let him give himself to serving" (Rom. 12:7) (AB). Could this not refer to those in special service as well as to laymen? Hence, it may be a call to pound a typewriter and answer a telephone in the pastor's office so that he can be released to better do his appointed service! Or it may be in a missionary society in the dusty office of a large city so that those called to foreign fields will not be forgotten, neglected, or destitute. It may even be in a dead-end job or a desk piled with boring routine tasks in a denominational headquarters. Are they not all part of the body?

If organizations are necessary, and they seem to be, then they have needs and these needs must be met. We have an example of this in a simple form when Jesus fed the five thousand (Luke 6:39, 40).

For these needs, *there can be* and *there is* the dignity of being *called of God.*

9
SHORT-TERM SERVICE

The discussion of short-term service is a delicate matter. The author confesses to having struggled considerably over how to deal with it. Should it be part of another subject already dealt with in previous chapters? Should it even be considered as a phase of the call of God?

An in-depth study resulted in the conclusion that short-term service cannot be overlooked. In fact it is of such profound importance that it was determined to give it full treatment in a chapter of its own.

BY WAY OF EXPLANATION

The term itself is self-explanatory. But, lest it be misconstrued and since it is the basis for some controversy, let us give our concept of what it encompasses before we consider its pros and cons and its important relationship to the call of God.

To begin with, and it should be made clear, short-term service, like special service, has no direct reference to the call to general service, which is inherent in salvation and primary to any subsequent call to special service (see Chapter 2).

Moreover, there is no contradiction between short-term service and special service if the use of the latter is preferred to the term full-time service. In fact short-term service is fundamentally *a distinctive phase of special service,* as will be elaborated later. It bears repeating and should be strongly reemphasized that special service does not refer to the person or his particular gifts or qualities but rather to a *type* of service. This is equally true of short-term service.

Short-term service, like special service, may be the result of the mystical, the circumstantial, or the organizational call, or a combination of any of these. It may be a call *for one particular isolated task* or be a *part of a lifetime occupation or vocation.*

Quite often it has strong reference to the mission field, whether in connection with independent or denominational mission boards. It need not, however, be strictly in this field alone. It might be a call to serve in one particular church or congregation or with some particular denomination or organization. It could be otherwise, for example, as an evangelist, an educator, or in another spiritual vocation.

BIBLICAL AUTHORITY

This approach to short-term service is adequately supported by the Bible. We hearken back to the story of Bezaleel and Aholiab. Not only was their call to special service an organizational type of call but it was also on a short-term basis. Once their work was done in the tabernacle, there was no further need for their services as far as Moses was concerned. It could reasonably be expected that they went back to their secular vocations.

Gideon's call was for one purpose and one purpose only. And the Lord looked at him and said, Go in this your strength and *deliver Israel* from the hand of Midian. Have I not sent you? (Judg. 6:14) (NASB).*

When Gideon had accomplished this and was offered the rulership over the Israelites, he refused. True, he is numbered among the judges of Israel, but his call was for special service as well as short-term service. When this was done, he had fulfilled all that God asked of him for that given purpose.

Luke relates the temporary mission of the seventy disciples (10:1). There is no evidence that they were all called into a continuing mission for Christ, though of that number twelve were chosen for special service as apostles.

There is the mission described by Matthew and Mark (Matt. 10; Mark 6) when the apostles were sent two by two on a specific journey through Galilee with instructions that were limited to that trip alone and were not applicable later!

Ananias who became God's mouthpiece and miracle-worker in Paul's historic call is introduced merely as "a certain *disciple* at Damascus" (Acts 9:10). In a few brief verses his "special service" to God is accomplished, and he passes from the scene, never to be heard from again. Paul's reference to him as "a devout man according to the law, having a good report of all the Jews" (Acts 22:12) and the fact that he was so signally used to put Paul on the right road to service for God certainly should have qualified him for greater and continued service. But not so! God's call to him for short-term service in the field of special service was fulfilled, as far as we know. It can safely be assumed that he continued to be a "devout" disciple doing general service.

There are others! "That brother (some assume this to be Luke) . . . was appointed by the churches to travel" (an organizational call found in 2 Cor. 8:18, 19) for the given

* Italics added.

purpose of securing an offering for the work of the gospel on a *short-term* basis.

Judas and Silas were "chosen men" selected by "the apostles and elders, with the whole church" (Acts 15:22) to accompany Paul and Barnabas with a *special* message for the church at Antioch. In their own rights and by their personal calling they "were themselves prophets (inspired interpreters of the will and purposes of God)" (Acts 15:32) (AB), but this was temporarily set aside for this special short-term service.

Certainly Paul's Macedonian Call on his second journey was temporary. He never did stay in Macedonia. After the mission was accomplished, he moved on.

THE LOYAL OPPOSITION

The very mention of short-term service to some is like waving a red flag before an angry bull. It sends the blood pressure skyrocketing and creates a storm of controversy. A basic reason for this is the deep-seated and well-meaning but greatly distorted philosophy that surrounds the idea of full-time service. The term itself, short-term service, some claim, is a contradiction of full-time service.

Possibly much of the opposition to this approach stems from those who are conditioned and belong to an autocratic system of government that equates obedience to leadership with obedience to God, and dedication to an organization with dedication to God. To disobey the leaders or to leave the organization is tantamount to disloyalty and desertion. In some extremes loyalty to the organization and its leaders is seemingly placed above loyalty to God. Such actions have brought ostracism and discrimination as well as created intolerable guilt for victims of such treatment.

Strangely enough, these same leaders and organizations never seem to object when those who leave other fields of service come to serve within *their* organization. Although they are quick to condemn the one who leaves them, they rejoice when another does the same thing and comes to serve within their particular sphere of service. In the first instance it is a case of reprobates who have fallen from grace, whereas in the second the newcomers are considered to be converts who have seen and come into the light.

However, the opposition from this source has been tempered somewhat in recent decades. Because of the change in political and spiritual climate and under the subsequent shortage in personnel, some organizations have become more flexible. Nonprofessional and nonordained persons have been used to take over the work and duties and even administrative responsibilities ordinarily assigned only to those who had ecclesiastical status. This is particularly true in professional fields where certain expertise is needed, but it is not totally restricted to them. Those with fewer professional skills have been equally employed. And much of this is done on a *short-term* basis. Need and expediency have altered and dictated these considerations.

Another source of opposition to short-term service comes from those who consider the so-called full-time service synonymous with lifetime service. They argue, if God called them to some particular field of service or location or to serve within an organization (with particular respect to their own, of course), then the responsive dedication must be *for life*. And, they further reason, if God called them to such, there can be no alterations or cessations since God never changes His mind.

The writer admits to having held and argued this philosophy for many years. However, the maturity of age along with increased knowledge and experience has taught the fallacy of such a rigid approach. True, God never changes His mind nor His ultimate will. But, since God exercises a permissive will,[1] His plan (not His mind) is altered to accomplish His ultimate purposes.

1. For an amplification of this vital subject, see Deratany, Edward: *Refuge In The Secret Place.* Glendale, Calif.: Gospel Light Publications, Regal Books, 1971 pp. 132-134.

Another argument against this philosophy is that when God calls a person to serve in a given geographic location, this must never change. A call to India or Africa is unalterable. But what if the door closes as it has in many countries? Paul was already a missionary when he heard the call, "Come over into Macedonia, and help us." This was merely further direction from the Lord and, simultaneously, it temporarily closed doors to Asia Minor. Now on a short-term stint he was ordered to take the gospel to Europe. He obeyed that call.

After the Communists took over China, one mission maintained a policy that all workers remain. Restricted to her home and not allowed to teach, one missionary wrote a letter of resignation to the board, "I can no longer remain since I was called to teach, not called to China. I must go where I can do what God called me to do."

Dr. Dick Hillis, General Director of Overseas Crusades, claims he was never called to China, although he served there as a missionary for eighteen years.

What about individuals who feel strongly called to one particular country but are sent by mission boards to another? The author has knowledge of several missionaries who have served in two or more countries where they were appointed by their denomination. In some instances they never even felt a call to the mission field. Adironam Judson was deeply burdened for India but served in Burma.

Such illustrations could be multiplied. Are they all in error, or is there a place for short-term service in given locations?

PRACTICAL SUPPORT

Richard Wolff, director of "Short Terms Abroad" comments and raises the following thought-provoking questions:

To assume that the missionary call is not subject to

change would be a denial and a limitation of the freedom of God who might wish to reassign the missionary (in His sovereignty) to another sphere of service. Should the missionary commit himself to a specific area for decades and become heedless to the possibility of an indication from the Holy Spirit to move to another country?

As Christians, we believe in *the priesthood of all believers*. Is the "missionary call" a specific call, the exclusive property of people working full time in the kingdom of God? Should not all Christians receive a vocational call? If so, does it mean that once engaged in the vocation, no changes should be undertaken—one would not even be free to leave the vocation for full-time Christian service, not to mention a change over to another vocation?

Do we expect every minister in the United States to have a call to a definite part of the country or to a specific church? Should the minister never leave this church or this part of the U.S.? Has it not happened that a minister has [been a candidate] in a church which has turned him down? Was there a misunderstanding on the part of the minister or on the part of the church? *Is it not a great temptation to take a temporary situation and to transform it into a permanent one? Was this not the temptation of Peter on the Mount of Transfiguration,* when he thought of building three tents? Was Jonah's call to Ninevah permanent?

It must be recognized that it has been *the actual experience of many persons that the call has, in fact changed. It could hardly be said of all those who were once on the mission field in obedience to specific calls, that regardless of the reason for their return to the homeland, they are now disobedient—including most mission executives!*

One of the strong arguments in favor of short-term service

is that it serves the purpose of giving guidance to those seeking direction as to God's purpose and will for them. Many denominations have for several years operated a type of service corps using older teens and young adults in home missions and abroad for a period of three months to two years. For many, starting from a basis of uncertainty, there has developed a conviction of God calling them to a specific vocation or a specific location. It was a graduation from short-term service in special service, to a lifetime of special service.

In some instances it has been God's crucible. The dross of half-hearted dedication and wrong motivation is removed under the heat of practical trials and testings. Was not this the experience of John Wesley who thought he was called to be a missionary to the Indians in America? Was this only a temporary call? Was he out of God's will? Did he misunderstand his call to the Indians? Howbeit, his return to Great Britain resulted in a monumental work and an exceptional revival that saved that country from the godless revolution that overran France.

Another point in favor of short-term service is observed in those dedicated Christians who are giving faithful full-time service *in secular occupations* but have never felt the call either to the mission field or to any other totally spiritual vocation. Although they find fulfillment and satisfaction in their own vocations, they feel a strong pull to give, in a sacrificial spirit, some of their talents and time to the direct service of God. Dare they be denied this opportunity for short-term service, which has proved to be beneficial both to them and to those whom they served?

Such is the story of Tom Uden, a skilled tradesman and a dedicated Christian, active as a leader in his local church and equally faithful in his secular vocation. One day, because of an unusual set of circumstances, he found himself facing an offer to use his expertise in a hospital operated by his denomination. To accept this position would result in considerably less income for him.

Could this be God's leading? He had always secretly envied those in the ministry. Often he had strongly desired such a vocation, but he waited for a call that never came. Now, past middle age, this organizational need presented itself. He reasoned that although he never felt the call to the ministry (could it be because of another mistaken concept of what that call is?), possibly he could give greater service to God through his skills and knowledge. The challenge became a call. At this writing Tom is finding satisfaction and giving glory to God in *short-term–special service* only because it came late in life.

THE HEART OF THE MATTER

The fears and opposition to short-term service are not all to be dismissed as without foundation. Certainly if God calls a person to serve within a specific organization, then loyalty and obedience to the lawful directives of its leaders are not to be dismissed at the whim and fancy of the one so called. Certainly, for everyone to do that which is right in his own eyes is to court chaos and disaster.

Nor is short-term service to be a convenience for those seeking adventure on an easy "merry-go-round" contract. Nor is it to be an escape hatch for the weak, the cowardly, or the self-seekers who want an out from the rigors of the lifetime vocation to which God has called them. Paul in his earlier prison epistles speaks of Demas as "my fellow-labourer" but ends grieving in his final epistle, "Demas hath forsaken me, having loved this present world" (2 Tim. 4:10). Nor is short-term service intended to be a palliative for those called to special service in the ministry or the mission field, a means of salving their conscience by a partial gift or half-consecration. There can be no bargains with God. It is not a question of either/or. The young man who said, "I'll give it a fling and if I don't like it . . . ," was already wrongly motivated. *And that is the heart of the matter!* "What does God want?" should be the criterion for the unqualified decision to be made.

Doing the work of God pleases God only if it is His will.

Has the Lord as much delight in burnt offerings and sacrifices
As in obeying the voice of the Lord?
Behold, to obey is better than sacrifice,
And to heed than the fat of rams (1 Sam. 15:22) (NASB).

There is a place in God's sovereign will for short-term service as well as lifetime special service but not for bargaining. He expects unqualified obedience!

10
BE SURE! HOW SURE?

When Jesus was fulfilling his ministry here on earth, He was challenged by the religious leaders on the source of his authority.

> And they kept saying to him, By what (sort of) authority are you doing these things, or who gave You this authority to do them? (Mark 11:28) (AB).

Earlier in His ministry, Matthew records of Christ: "For He was teaching as [One] Who had [and was] authority." Moreover, He went so far in His ministry as to claim for Himself: "The Son of Man has authority on earth to forgive sins" (Luke 5:24).

Although Jesus did not give an outright answer to the leaders of His day, He did declare to His disciples later at Galilee, "All authority has been given to me in heaven and on earth" (Matt. 28:18) (NASB). This was said as a prelude to issuing the Great Commission, which constituted *the transfer of authority* to the apostles and to all succeeding disciples.

THE CALL IS AUTHORITY

The servant of God today, as with Christ and Paul, needs some authority for his vocation in special service. Like His Savior, he should be able to say, "The Spirit of the Lord is upon me, because the Lord hath anointed and qualified me to preach the Gospel" (Isa. 61:1) (AB). These words identified Christ with the prophets of the past, and this anointing was the basis for His authority.

Paul in writing to Titus declared, "These things speak, and exhort, and rebuke *with all authority.*" Another version puts it "urge (advise, encourage, warn) and rebuke *with full authority*" (Titus 2:15) (AB). Having admonished Titus and others to use the authority that was given them, Paul indicated the source for such authority, "There is no authority except from God—by His permission, His sanctions; and those that exist do so by God's appointment" (Rom. 13:1) (AB). He further claimed that same authority from the same source for himself and for his fellow ministers:

> (It is He) Who has qualified us (making us to be fit and worthy and sufficient) as ministers and dispensers of a new covenant (of salvation through Christ) (2 Cor. 3:6a) (AB).
>
> For (the proclaiming of) this (Gospel), I was *appointed* a herald (preacher) and an apostle (special messenger) and a teacher (of the Gentiles) (2 Tim. 1:11) (AB).

Incidentally, note the combination of the three types of special service to which he is called: herald, apostle, and teacher.

John Murray comments on another reference to Paul's claim to authority,

> Call and apostleship go together; it is by call that he became an apostle. And the call is the effectual appoint-

ment by which he was invested with the apostolic functions. It is the consciousness of authority derived from this appointment that alone explains and warrants the authority with which the apostle spoke and wrote.

Separated unto the gospel of God is parallel to "called to be an apostle " [1] (Rom. 1:1).

Agnew has this to say about the same scripture,

"Called"—this is literally "constituted," or "appointed." As it is likely that no apostle had established the church at Rome, there was much need of one with authority to declare unto them the whole gospel of God. As Paul declares himself to be "separated unto the gospel," it is well to remember that separation is never isolation; it is insulation.[2]

It has already been pointed out that youths are constantly being urged to dedicate their lives to special service. With this admonition they are given that sincere but sometimes vague or misguiding caution: "Be sure you are called!" If theirs could be the unusual, mystical type of call, well and good—there would be no problem. It is regrettable that out of an interpretation of Scripture there has developed this "crisis" approach to the call. But since a large percentage of Christian youth are "noncrisis" oriented and since this type of call comes only to a limited few, many remain puzzled over the questions, "How can I be sure?" or "What is the call?" Inasmuch as the call is the basis for authority, Scripturally speaking, this cannot be ignored or shunted to one side.

1. Murray, John: *The Epistle to the Romans.* Edited by Charles Hodge. New York: Wm. B. Eerdmans Publishing Co., 1950, p. 13. Used by permission.

2. Agnew, Milton S.: *More than Conquerors.* New York: Salvation Army National Information Service, 1959, p. 13.

To attempt to perform the sacred functions of an evangelist without the deep conviction of a call would lead to profanity and failure. No one can stand the strain of living up to so high a vocation without the spiritual resources needed to execute its demands. Is there a more pathetic sight than to watch someone struggling to "hold down" a job for which there has been no divine endowment? [3]

LEARNING THE WILL OF GOD

In previous paragraphs we have mentioned God's plan for our salvation and sanctification and, simultaneously, our call to general service as part of God's will. This has been established for *all* Christians. But the matter of special service is something more. To each must come that *personal* and *positive confirmation* of what the will of God is in this particular area.

One great leader presenting a challenge in a youth conference declared, "The call of God deals with the physical location. God could have used Abraham in Ur, *but* God wanted him in Canaan." Another leader seemingly minimized the geographic location by writing, "It makes no difference whether I am in China or America," and stressed the use of the gifts God has given. Although there appears to be a conflict in philosophy, it really doesn't exist. Either of these men would readily admit that *the will of God* is the *supreme* substance. In fact, the latter went on to write, "I must get my direction where to use that gift. . . . I must learn His will and do it." To this we would add, if God calls to some particular place or some particular endeavor, *that* is of greatest significance and that is where we must be or what we must do, if we would obey the call and be in His will. It is of paramount importance if we would experience His favor.

3. Smith, George B.: *The War Cry.*

As stated previously, for some there is no problem. The mystical call identifies the will of God and this conclusion is reached with simplicity. For many others, there is that element of uncertainty. Honestly and earnestly, they grasp for that nod of approval, for that sense of authority that in essence says, "I am here and occupied because God has chosen me." But *how* do they come to this positive assurance?

We have already established that since each individual is unique, God will deal with each person *where he is* and in keeping with *who he is!* His approach will be on an individual basis. No two persons see precisely the same view from any window. No two men hear particularly the same sounds. Therefore, no single pattern can be the answer to the question, "How can I know the will of God?"

On the other hand, there is one great and comforting answer that can be given to this desperate cry—God *will* make *His will* and *His way* known to every sincere seeker.

> I will instruct thee and teach thee in the way thou shalt go; I will guide thee with mine eye (Ps. 32:8).
>
> Rely with all your heart on the Eternal, and never lean on your own insight; have mind of Him wherever you may go, and He will clear the road for you (Prov. 3:5, 6) (Moffatt).

Many anxious, godly leaders and counselors have offered excellent suggestions on how to learn the will of God. Using a composite of these, the following sections are submitted alliteratively with the prayer that it may help youths and their counselors to learn the will of God for themselves. Bear in mind, and it cannot be overstressed, there is no exact blueprint that God uses after which any life will be patterned or by which God will reveal His will. Although much has already been written about vocations, both secular and spiritual, it would be profitable to add that for the true

Christian seeking the will of God and particularly for those entering special service, the call makes the basic difference between these vocations and merely having a job or seeking a career. The latter is *self-motivated,* whereas the former are *God-inspired.* This is most obvious from Scripture references quoted here. This is why we must know His will.

Seek.

Earnestly seek the will of God. Deeply involved in the search for discovering God's will is motivation. It is unlikely that God will reveal His plan for you if you are not interested enough to search out God's mind for your future.

Remember that any call of God will always be synonymous with the will of God. Therefore, there must be a *determined* effort to *learn* this will of God. Do this with the conviction that God not only has a plan for your life but will also lead you to a knowledge of His plan.

We are told that young people today have 50,000 careers from which to choose. Pressures from many sources make it difficult to make the proper choice. In fact, at times, the decision seems almost impossible. Yet God never intends that you should fly blindly into the future. Even as Jesus claimed authority and then transferred it to the apostles through the Great Commission, so your call, as you seek the will of God, will come and constitute your authority.

The personal approach of God's call will always be a mystery. Leave it with Him. He will make His plan and His will known to you. A brief review of the story of Philip, Jonah, and Paul reveals that God said "Go!" but He also said "Don't go!" If you have any sensitivity to God, you will rest most comfortably in the promise,

And your ears will hear a word behind you, this is the way, walk in it, whenever you turn to the right or to the left (Isa. 30:21) (NASB).

Search.

It hardly seems necessary to urge the exercise of prayer and Bible reading. Surprisingly enough though, many youths (and even adult Christians) do little to pursue these means of communication with God. They are an absolute essential to learning the will of God and should be regarded as standard equipment for the seeker of God's will. These exercises should become a part of your personality, a part of all you seek to do so that through His Word, God can counsel you. When these primary and basic steps are followed, God will not allow you to walk in darkness. He will not even allow you to err, if you are keenly sensitive to His Holy Spirit and do not force your will on His. To put it simply, if not profoundly:

> The will of God
> will never lead ya'
> Where the grace of God
> cannot keep ya'.

Paul the Apostle, though before his conversion diametrically opposed to God's will and plan, was so deeply immersed in the Scriptures and in prayer (ritualistic though it may have been) that he could, at His call, immediately respond to God's voice, "Who are you, Lord?" Drawing on His past knowledge, while still in Damascus, he "put to confusion the Jews . . . by comparing and examining evidence (Scripture) and proving that Jesus is the Christ, the Messiah" (Acts 9:22) (AB).

T. Norton Sterrett condenses God's different methods of calling (only for Christians) to three types, the Word of God, the impressions of prayer, and the circumstances of life. They may, he claims, be used individually or collectively, but eventually all three will agree. Describing these, he wisely cautions:

Don't depend on circumstances alone to show you God's will. Why? Because at first they may indicate the opposite. They may be obstacles to test your faith, your persistence. So lean your weight on the guidance of the Word of God and the voice of the Holy Spirit in prayer. Trust the voice of circumstances only for confirmation.[4]

As an illustration of his position, Sterrett quotes C. T. Studd's testimony, from the Norman P. Grubb biography:

"About this time I met with a tract written by an atheist." This tract told what the atheist thought he would do with his life if he really believed what Christians said they believed. The conviction that came with the reading so compelled Studd that he says, "I therefore determined that from that time forth my life should be consistent. *I set myself to know what was God's will for me.*" This was the channel of circumstances.

The voice of God came through the second means a little later, as testified in these words: "I had felt that England was big enough for me. But now my mind seemed constantly to run in the direction of the Lord's work abroad." This was the agency of impressions through prayer.

Further uncertainties troubled Studd, and they were resolved as God spoke in a third way. The experience was this: "I prayed to God to guide me by His Word. I felt that there was one thing alone which could keep me from going, and that was the love of my mother; but I read that passage 'He that loveth father or mother more than me is not worthy of me' after which I knew it was God's will and I decided to go." [5]

4. From *Called of God—and Sure of It* by T. Norton Sterrett. Copyright © 1949 by Inter-Varsity Christian Fellowship and used by permission of Inter-Varsity Press.

5. *Ibid.,* pp. 8, 9.

In your search for God's will, don't look for handwriting on the wall or letters in the clouds. Just talk to God through prayer, and let Him talk to you through the Bible. He may use inner or outer means, the obvious or subtle—leave it to Him. He'll come through clear and plain!

Study.

Don't underestimate yourself! Many a youth looks at some spiritual giant, a great Bible character or his own pastor or leader and draws away with the defeatist attitude "I just don't have it." Unfortunately, there is an inclination to think that God chooses only select people as though they were ready-made and eager to jump in, full force, to the service God calls them. Quite the contrary!

A quick look at Moses as he gazed into the burning bush reminds us of his lack of confidence shown by his negative reply to God's call, "Who am I that I should go?" (Gen. 3:11).

Gideon, equally lacking in confidence, answered God's call, "O Lord, how shall I deliver Israel? . . . I am the youngest in my father's house" (Judg. 6:15) (NASB).

These are typical of many—all around us today. The call is no less real, the struggle is not less real, and the response of faith and love is as hesitant as of old. But it *need not* be! It *must not* be!

One thing is sure—your real abilities are something only God knows. Discovering yourself under the Spirit's illumination can be the thrill of a lifetime. Many a man who could never picture himself a prophet is today doing things he never dreamed possible.

Surrender of your inadequacies real or imagined, as well as your material prospects—again real or imagined —is an indispensable prerequisite to discovering God's will for you.[6]

6. Read, Edward: *The Crest.* Reprinted from *The Crest,* the Salvation Army's Youth Magazine for Canada and Bermuda.

If a person is looking for excuses because of an unwilling spirit or for a coward's refuge, he has an ally. Satan is anxious to cooperate most fully and can furnish all the excuses desired. He loves nothing better.

For instance, in the present atmosphere of affluence and materialism he persuasively suggests, "Why not enter some lucrative business, enterprise, or profession that would pay more? Then you could offer your family a better chance in life and give you a better advantage. After all, you can serve God equally as well in that field, as in being a preacher, a missionary . . . !"

To these and other rationalizations there can be only one answer—to do God's work is not necessarily to do God's will. The only criterion is the will of God, nothing more, nothing less, nothing else. Dr. Ted W. Engstrom put it this way:

> Being a Christian is a vocation in itself, so actually *every* Christian is in full-time service whether he be a preacher or a farmer. Your decision is not "Shall I go into Christian service?" but "In what vocation can I best serve the Lord with the talents He has given me?"

If, on the other hand, circumstances and a lack of ability or knowledge are actually present when the call comes, then that is God's responsibility. He will either furnish, guide in securing, or overrule in the need because of the inadequacies.

> God hath chosen the foolish things of the world to confound the wise; and God hath chosen the weak things of the world to confound the things which are mighty. And base things of the world, and things which are despised, hath God chosen, yea and things which are not, to bring to nought things that are.
> That no flesh should glory in His presence (1 Cor. 1:27–29).

Mind you, the value of an honest self-evaluation is not to be underestimated. Determine your own abilities, your likes and dislikes, your strengths and your weaknesses. Tests and counselling with pastors and leaders will help to objectively uncover your potentials and weaknesses. One writer has stated, "I believe your calling and gift are identical. Your call is what you are to be, which is determined by the gift He has given you." *This is not altogether true.* God may use the gifts He has already given to reveal His will. On the other hand, many have been called to serve in a field for which they had no aptitude or desire, but God gave gifts *after* that calling came. One of the benefits of self-evaluation is the awareness of needs that should be acquired or developed. Phillips Brooks resigned as a teacher since he had no control over the students. *After three years of training,* he went into the ministry and became one of the world's greatest preachers. Additionally, he blessed the world with his song, "O Little Town of Bethlehem." He failed as a teacher but succeeded in his true calling.

In the final analysis, whom God calls, He uses! Whom He uses, He equips. The only qualification He wants is a willing and an obedient spirit. David Riley, after reviewing the manuscript of this book, capsuled the heart of this matter beautifully with the comment, "The call is divine. The doubts are human. God resolves the doubts."

The sage counsel of Canon J. Stafford Wright is a fitting conclusion to this section:

My advice is that, if a man is capable of taking a degree, whether or not it is in theology, he should take the best class that he can. If he is not capable of a degree, the selection body of his Church will advise him what he can do. There is no need for a feeling of inferiority. If one looks at the records of some of the ministers whom God has used very greatly, one will find they are without degrees. Yet this does not mean that a man would be right to refuse to read [study] for a degree if he is capable of taking one, for then he might well be interfering with the pattern of God's calling for him.

There is no need to be in a hurry. For some it is right to go straight from school or university to a theological college, but a year or two in a job of some kind is a tremendous asset. If in the meantime one discovers that the Lord is opening up avenues of service as a Christian layman, then weigh up the call to ordination afresh, One cannot say how, but certainly *God will make it clear to a man whether He is calling him to the ordained ministry now, later, or not at all.*[7]

Submit.

In seeking God's will, it is most important that you have a *yielded will.* Ever and always there should be established in your own mind, "I have no will of my own in this matter." If you are already choosing what *you* will do for God, you are already frustrating God's will. Your will must be totally subservient to God Who takes the initiative both in claiming us for His own and then appointing us to His service. Lyell Rader, Sr., has characteristically stated, "For a Christian to assert his own will in opposition to the mind of Christ is not just crazy, it is high treason."

If you decide that you prefer music, or teaching, or law, or any other vocation *without consulting God,* you are violating the sovereignty of God. If God is really God, He has the right to speak in imperatives. What you would *like* is not the question to be settled. The problem is: *What does God want?*

To be absolutely obedient and consecrated is the only touchstone to the will of God. To do so you must conform

7. Joyce, C. A., editor: *My Call to the Ministry.* London: Marshall, Morgan & Scott, 1968, p. 124. Used by permission. Italics added.

to the challenge of Paul, ". . . Present your bodies a living sacrifice, holy, acceptable unto God which is your reasonable service" (Rom. 12:1). The personification of this is typified by Kipling's Mulholland. While working on a cattle boat, he was converted during a storm at sea:

> An' by the terms of the contract, as I have
>   read the same,
> If He got me to port alive I would exalt
>   His name,
> An' praise His Holy Majesty till further
>   orders came.

Further orders came and were "back you go to the cattle boats an' preach My gospel there."

> I didn't want to do it, for I knew what
>   I should get,
> An' I wanted to preach religion, handsome
>   an' out of the wet,
> But the word of the Lord were lain on me,
>   an' I done what I was set.

Serve.

Those strange stirrings, those strong emotions, those intense desires are not to be dismissed lightly. There are those who would play down emotions as a criterion for the Call of God. It may be possible that sometimes a desire may be more of an emotional drive than the explicit will of God. We must guard against this. However, we must never minimize the importance of emotions. We *are* emotional beings, and God uses the emotions as channels through which he communicates to us. In fact, emotions are quite relevant to the business of God—a prerequisite to the ministry. A true love for God, stirred up by the Holy Spirit, will show itself in a true love for men, for lost souls. How often it was said of Jesus, that He looked on (them) with compassion. Our love, at best, is but a reflection of His for us.

Therefore, a strong feeling of unrest, *a strong desire to serve* God in some particular field, or any other stirring of the emotions could well be the voice of God—God's call to you. *Get busy for the Lord!* Start moving in whatever direction doors open to you. If you feel led to preach, start preaching.

But we are also rational beings. To lean only on the emotions is as dangerous as to ignore them. God also speaks to the intellect and balances the one with the other. As a boy on the farm, I had a team of horses that were harnessed together. One of the horses was inclined to hold back, allowing the other to move ahead. In order to get the best results, it was necessary to prod the laggard with a whip. This may be true with us, and God may have to chastise us either emotionally or mentally to bring us into His full plan.

However, to allow emotions to dominate is likely to lead to fanaticism. Conversely, if the intellect is the strongest pull, rigid formalism can occur. God needs a balance of both to get the hay, and the wheat, and the other harvest in "while it is yet day."

But we are quick to add, keep all this in the context of what has been emphasized heretofore, with the repeated stress not to expect a blinding flash or a thundering voice. If God chooses this type of call, well and good. If not, *start walking* in the direction you think or feel He is directing. And *keep walking until He closes doors.* Better to err in the direction He seems to lead than to stand around idly waiting for a blinding, flashing light.

Warning: Be prepared for God's detours. Undesirable, inconvenient, and unexpected, these pop up at us when we travel life's highways. The Wise Men at the nativity of Jesus, "being warned in a dream not to return to Herod, they departed to their own country by another way" (Matt. 2:12). *Detour!* Christ Himself could have traveled the way of ease, popularity, and power but God's will for Him was the cross. *Detour!* Paul wanted Asia, but God said "Macedonia." *Detour!*

Lyell Rader, Sr., referring to Paul's detour, suggests a unique and an excellent pattern in traveling and facing detours:

> The Bible, in Acts 19:9, 10, explains why Paul was "forbidden of the Holy Ghost to preach the word in Asia." The Master strategist had planned for that area to be covered by Paul's converts. The Spirit also bypassed Bythinia and needed only to show Paul the greater need of Macedonia and away he went without question "assuredly gathering that the Lord had called." Paul needed a compass needle to pinpoint the greatest need and God's choice for him.

The elements which comprise the guidance of God are evident in Paul's experience:

1. *He heeded God's general orders.* He was busy winning souls, following God's general guidance as recorded in His word.
2. *His was a yielded will.* He was *able to take "no" for an answer.* One might as well put a wad of chewing gum on the compass needle as to expect guidance when the will is already set, the mind made up. Human judgment is a wonderfully sensitive and accurate faculty when yielded to and adjusted by the Creator. However, there is nothing more perverse when it is biased by sin, self, and Satan. It should be said, in this connection, that *prayer ought not to be a struggle to overcome God's reluctance but a loving search to discover God's willingness.*

3. *He recognized providential circumstances in the en-counter with Lydia's prayer circle.*

The sure guidance of God is obtained when these factors—the *written Word, sanctified judgment,* and *providential circumstances—coincide.* God will not guide us one way by His Word and another way by His Spirit. Military control centers use a method of verification known as "triangulation." A single plotting is not acceptable if three can be obtained. For example, if the propeller of an enemy submarine is picked up by sonar, the nearest three stations are plotted. If their directional signals pass through a common point, there is no question as to the position of that sub.

If the three factors outlined agree as you contemplate them in repeated prayer, your heart and mind will be *kept* (protected and preserved from attack) by "the peace of God which passeth all understanding." If this peace persists, never fear; assuredly gather that the Lord has called. *"Peace" is the final compass needle.*[8]

Sit still.

These were the words Naomi gave to Ruth after she had done all she could to bring about what later proved to be God's plan and will.

Sit still . . . until thou know how the matter will fall (Ruth 3:18).

Oftentimes this is more difficult than being engaged in a frenzy of activities. But sometimes this is most important. If the answer to prayer—the call from God—doesn't come when it should, Be patient! God wants to make your life

8. Lyle Rader, Sr., *The War Cry.*

count the most for His glory. Trust Him to do the right thing at the right time. His delays may be a test.

Possibly, at this juncture, it would be helpful to list Hannah Whitehall Smith's formula [9] (one among many) for ascertaining God's leading:

1. Scriptures
2. Providential circumstances
3. Convictions of our own higher judgment
4. Inward impressions of the Holy Spirit

The last is best experienced when we are "quiet before the Lord."

Finally, as for one particular spiritual leader and perhaps for you, the call may be progressive: first, *a possibility,* very faint, then, *a probability,* a stage in which you alternate between convictions and queries, finally, a *certainty.*

The Call of God

These words what strange illusions to the
    mind
Are brought to those who would their all
    present
Were it not for the vagueness of the line.

The words do conjure up
A sense ethereal to some,
Who fain would follow, doubting nought
    except
The thought that this voice first should
    come.

9. Smith, Hannah Whitehall: *The Christian's Secret of a Happy Life.* Boston: G. K. Hall, 1973, p. 95.

Certain, sure, at last,
Conviction in the soul will grow
No other path can satisfaction bring.
Preach I must, or great will be my woe.

Disciple young and strong,
Wait not till life has run its course
Before presenting Christ just what is left.
A living sacrifice: or else remorse!

Your life is precious now;
The world around you calls in trust.
Undone the task, or sinners leave in sin—
Alternate choice? Present your all to
    Christ! [10]

Geoffrey Perry

10. Perry, Geoffrey: *The Officer,* 1965, p. 101.

11
STOP! LOOK! AND LISTEN

A young man, trying to carry on a conversation from a telephone booth located on a busy thoroughfare, kept repeating, "I can't hear you! I can't hear you!" Eventually, the party on the other end of the line, hearing the din of the street traffic and sensing the cause of the problem, said, "If you will close the door, you will be able to hear me." How typical of some who would know the will of God but experience confusion because of the clatter and competition of noises and voices of the world around them. A determined effort to shut out this competition and to concentrate on the voice of God would so easily and quickly clarify the spiritual audition.

A similiar story is told of two men, the elder of whom was urging upon the younger the claim of Christian work and encouraging him to follow the call of the Lord.

The younger answered with an excuse that had a familiar ring: "But I have never received a call."

"Are you sure you are within calling distance?" was the disquieting reply.

ESPECIALLY LISTEN!

Up to this point, we have dealt with the subject of the call of God from the position of those who would earnestly seek and know the mind of God—those who would *welcome the call* to special service—if they could recognize it. Hopefully, we have covered this adequately so that as these problems are encountered, a solution may be found.

There are others to whom God calls but who for one reason or another tend to turn Him off. By the manipulation of Satan and his employed devices, a barrier is created so that God can't get through. The alluring sirens of pleasure, the cooing call for comfort, the press for popularity, the hawking vendors of materialism, the endless pressures for position and education, and a hundred other voices create such a cacophony that the voice of God seems all but lost.

The time-honored railroad warning is apropos in such circumstances. If disaster would be averted and if the ultimate of God's blessing be experienced, such persons would do well to *Stop! Look!* and (especially) *Listen!* God will speak. But He seeks a listening ear.

There are two areas—traps—into which those whom we refer to in this chapter are ensnared.

RIGHT MOTIVE—WRONG VOICE

The first of these traps is the category of those who earnestly seek to serve God but hear and heed the wrong voices. They listen to the philosophy that "you can do just as well or even more for God as a layman, right where you are" in opposition to the call of God to special service. They are impressed with the argument that everybody wants to accomplish something worthwhile in the world and to choose special service is to lack respectablity among those with whom they live. To do Christian service as a minister, an evangelist, or a missionary is to be marked as slightly strange. It is much more respectable to be a doctor, lawyer, or schoolteacher. In other words, they become conditioned to think that being separated for the ministry is a subcalling or for those who are "not quite so sharp." Much better to serve in respected secular fields and use your Christian influence from these elevated positions.

Although this may seem to be true and valid for some, it is not so if the voice of God calls otherwise.

Finding respectability in the eyes of human beings may be important. Finding respectability in the eyes of God is infinitely more important.

Bishop James K. Mathews points out that the "ministry of the laity" has been blamed for undercutting vocations to the ministry. He insists that what he terms (in support of our original premise) "full-time Christian service" is an obligation resting on all Christians, but that these same Christians must recognize that a fully staffed ministry is the responsibility of the whole church.

"If the church is to attract recruits for its ministry, it will be necessary for this role to be seen again as 'significant' in our culture," says Bishop Mathews. He raps the distortion of "the current stereotype of the Protestant minister, fostered by Hollywood and New York cartoons—an underpaid, over-worked, 'pious' long-faced, milk-toast, effeminate sort of person. This is manifestly unfair and grossly distorted."

Also competing are the voices that suggest legitimate and proper reasons for choosing other than God's will. They convincingly argue that duty at home, the needs of local situations, and similar services are just as important as the ministry. The contention that it is wrong to waste one's life in barren fields when there is so much to be done right where you are is plausible. The question still remains, "Whose voice is speaking and to whom are you listening?"

David Rees' testimony illustrates this point:

Six months after my conversion the Spirit of God made it plain to me that I ought to apply for Officership in the

Salvation Army; but at this time I was entirely responsible for the support of a widowed mother and an invalid sister, the only other person in the house being a younger brother who was given to drink and worldliness.

I tried hard to make myself believe I was mistaken and *that God would never call me from home under existing circumstances.* I conferred with several Christian people outside The Army, who, I thought, would know the mind of God better than a young convert like myself. *They assured me that I was all wrong in supposing that God would ever call a young man to leave home who was responsible for his parent as I was.*

In spite of all this, however, the conviction grew upon me, as born of God, that at all cost I must follow His call, and all my heart was set to win souls. I prayed, I think I may say without ceasing, and eventually I made known my feelings to my mother. She said she would sooner die in the workhouse than stand in the way of my following what I believed to be a call of God, and rejoiced my heart by adding that this was the least she could do out of gratitude to God and The Army for my salvation.

Still I struggled against the conviction. The more I thought of leaving her, the more I realized my love for my widowed mother as days and months went by. The great trial which came very forcibly to me at times was that she would be exposed to privation and want without me. I believed that God was able and would take care of His own, and yet it seemed a terrible thing to go and simply leave her. But after waiting about twelve months, I volunteered. I could delay no longer.

In due course, the Sunday came for me to say farewell at my Corps. On the Sunday night, my brother, who was directly opposed to all religion . . . entered the Army hall for the first time, with my sister, and at the close of the meeting both volunteered for salvation. I shall never forget my feelings when I saw them at the Mercyseat.

Then and there my brother publicly confessed Christ and, what is more, undertook the entire responsibility of my widowed mother and home, and that responsibility he has faithfully and lovingly discharged.

God's faithfulness has been verified in my experience over and over again in quite as marked a manner, and I believe that in making that first consecration in faith for my loved ones I learned, perhaps, the greatest lesson of my life. In many severe and dark trials and losses it has helped me to stay myself on God. It set a seal on my call to officership, which has been more to me than anything that man could do for me.

RIGHT VOICE—WRONG MOTIVE

Far more pathetic is the situation where the individual, knowing the will of God, either *seeks* special service or *avoids* it *for personal reasons.*

These fit into the category of either the Ananiases and Sapphiras of the early church (Acts 5:1–11) or the chief rulers who feared to confess Christ because they "loved the praise of men more than the praise of God" (John 12:43). Sometimes their motives are affected by materialism—either the desire for or the lack of it. Security is also a powerful influence, both the desire for security or the fear of insecurity in response to the call of God.

Geoffrey I. Treglown candidly admits, "I became a preacher and a minister for all the wrong reasons." At the age of five, the idea flashed into his mind that if he was to be good and go to heaven, he must be a minister like his grandfather. Innocently misled by the opinions and flattery of others, he began preaching at the age of fourteen—not truly knowing a conversion experience with God. For a number of years his life was a mixture of not only a desire to serve God and people but also of shallow ambitions and disillusionments. Realizing his spiritual poverty, he eventually recognized his motives for what they were, experienced a positive Christian experience, and now continues his life with a positive testimony.

Dr. Dwight E. Loder of Garrett Theological Seminary denounces the church when it employs surface attractions to the ministry, judging them as both misleading and improper. He charges that too often the church attempts to recruit its ministry using the lures of the secular world: security, material gain, success, comfort, status, power, and influences. This, he contends, is belittling to the ministry and does not attract strong and able people to it. Summarily he declares, "The ministry cannot tolerate and the church cannot survive a ministry operating on secular standards."

The individual who obeys the call of God for self-seeking purposes must either have his values refined or court disaster. Even though the world's respectability and security may seem essential to the present and the future, there is no guarantee that these will abide. There is no greater calling under God; there is no greater security; there is no greater privilege in the world than to have God speak and say,

> Ye have not chosen me but I have chosen you, and ordained you, that ye shall go and bring forth fruit, and that your fruit should remain: that whatsoever ye shall ask of the Father in My name, He may give it to you (John 15:16).

Sacrifice is and must be the hallmark of the followers of Christ. Once again, the profound philosophy of William Booth supports a point for us:

> *"Going means leaving."* You can't go to all the world without leaving something—something that flesh and blood would like to keep, something that perhaps, apart from saving the world, flesh and blood would have a right to keep; but which flesh and blood gladly give up.

And so for you to go means leaving some father and mother, or sweetheart or someone who objects, who will count you a fool or a madman.

THE HOUND OF HEAVEN

While God will not lower Himself to the level of being a competitor with the other voices, yet in His graciousness and love He does not readily and easily forsake us when we demur or balk at His call. He knows well the enemy of His plan and of those whom He calls. Rather than exercise His omnipotence and impose His sovereign will or leave us to our ill-chosen fate, He *invites* us to "come now and let us reason together" (Isa. 1:18). He allows an Abraham to plead for mercy on the basis of fifty righteous souls; then forty-five, forty, thirty, twenty, and even ten (Gen. 18:23–33).

If we deliberately and conclusively sin away our day of grace and close the door on ourselves, as far as God's call is concerned, then the consequences must be ours. But as long as there is a vestige of hope, in spite of any flaw in our dedication or our exercise of escape mechanisms, God pursues us with an intent that is beyond human understanding. His persistence in what Albert Orsborn terms "the disturbing call of God" brings about periods of restlessness, dissatisfaction, a sense of "something wrong in my life" until there comes the resolution of the unrest when at last I give in and cry out, "Lord, what wilt thou have me to do?" (Acts 9:6).

George Matheson, in the spirit of the stirring thought of "The Hound of Heaven," penned his immortal song:

> O Love that will not let me go,
> I rest my weary soul in thee;

> I give Thee back the life I owe,
>   That in Thine ocean depths its
>   flow
>   May richer, fuller be.

THEN GO!

To restate the railroad slogan in the childhood jingle of yesteryears:

> Stop! Look! and Listen!
>   Before you cross the street
> Use your eyes, use your ears
>   Then use your feet.

The soul attuned to God will unquestionably hear the voice of God. He may not know totally God's plan, but God will know the direction in which He wants him to move. The classic response to this is our example:

> By faith Abraham, when he was *called to go* into a place which he should after receive for an inheritance, obeyed; *and he went out, not knowing whither he went* (Heb. 11:8).*

Abraham knew no goal, he had no mission, he acted only with obedience and faith. In modern parlance he acted by giving God a blank check endorsed by himself and left it up to the Divine to fill in the amount. Even as every act of God is the outcome of unlimited love for man, so true obedience is the outcome of true love to Christ and is the measure of our love.

John Larsson recognizes and grapples with this very basic problem. In many ways he skillfully capsules much of what

* Italics added.

has been written here. His main thesis is that by the ordinary method of presenting the call we have created a dichotomy of two calls—the passive and the active. The first of these is predominant and says, "I am chosen." In this instance, man is a puppet and moves at the Master's bidding. Larsson complains that "we lose many potential officers [ministers] by a far too narrow presentation of 'the call.' " [1] He suggests that we make available to young people who feel they *ought* to give their lives for God's service and *do not want to do it,* a ready-made loophole.

The other side of the coin, the active call, begins with the call of God to *all* His children and to total commitment. The concept of "stewardship involvement" is deeply ingrained in man, and to God's slightest nudge he responds with "How can I better serve Thee, Lord?" This total commitment prevailing in the general call will, for some, perhaps many, lead into the special service of subsequent calls.

In his thesis, Larsson logically concludes by pointing out that it is not an either/or proposition between the active or passive calls. Rather it is both, and these two strands can be reconciled.

Referring again to the words of Paul (Rom. 1:1) about being "separated [or set apart] unto the gospel of God," we find support for the position that Larrson claims and we have endorsed, from the following:

The separation here spoken of does not refer to the predestination of Paul to the office, as in Gal. 1:15, but to the *effectual dedication* that occurred in the actual call to the apostleship and indicates what is entailed in the call. No language could be more eloquent of *the decisive action of God* and of *the completeness of Paul's resulting commitment* to the gospel. *All bonds of interest and at-*

1. Larrson, John: "How Comes the Call?" *The Officer,* 1965, p. 101.

tachment alien and extraneous to the promotion of the gospel have been cut asunder and he is set apart by the investment of all his interest and ambitions in the cause of the gospel. It is, of course, implied that the gospel as a message is to be proclaimed and, if we were to understand the "gospel" as the actual proclamation, *dedication to this proclamation would be an intelligible and worthy conception.* However, the word "gospel" is not used in the sense of the act of proclaiming: it is the message proclaimed. And this is stated to be the "gospel of God" (cf. Mark 1:14). The stress falls upon the divine origin and character of the gospel. It is a message of glad tidings from God, and it never loses its divinity, for it ever continues to be God's message of salvation to lost men.[2]

John Oxenham poetically translates the heart of this chapter in one of his masterpieces:

Follow Me

Lord, I would follow, but—
First, I would see what means
    that wondrous call
That peals so sweetly through
    Life's rainbow hall,
That thrills my heart with
    quivering golden chords,
And fills my soul with joys
    seraphical.

Lord, I would follow, but—
First, I would leave things
    straight before I go,

---

2. Murray, John: *The Epistle to the Romans.* Edited by Charles Hodge. New York: Wm. B. Eerdmans Publishing Co., 1950, p. 3. Used by permission. Italics added.

Collect my dues and pay
   the debts I owe;
Lest when I'm gone, and none
   is here to tend,
Time's ruthless hand my
   garnering o'erthrow.

Lord, I would follow, but—
First, I would see the end of
   this high road
That stretches straight before
   me, fair and broad;
So clear the way I cannot go
   astray
It surely leads me equally to
   God.

Lord, I would follow—yea,
Follow I will, but first so
   much there is
That claims me in life's vast
   emergencies,
Wrongs to be righted, great
   things to be done;
Shall I neglect these vital
   urgencies?

Who answers Christ's insistent call
Must give himself, his life, his all,
Without one backward look.
Who sets his hand unto the plow,
And glances back with anxious brow,
His calling hath mistook.
Christ claims him wholly for his own;
He must be Christ's, and Christ's alone.[3]

3. Morrison, James Dalton: *Masterpieces of Religious Verse*. New York: Harper & Row, Publishers, 1948.

12

CONFIRMATION OF THE CALL

"But I'm still not sure!" This honest cry of anguish from the lips of earnest souls seeking a definite word of assurance carries with it the unspoken, plaintive plea, "Can you help me?"

There is nothing so devastating to the mind and spirit as a prolonged feeling of uncertainty. It seems logical and reasonable that God should resolve any doubt and confirm a personal call to special service when it is in harmony with His will. Moreover, it is spiritually logical to maintain that to sustain a ministry in freshness and power through the years, a person must not only know a divine call but be convinced of its validity.

The motives for undertaking special service may not initially be high or holy and may even be mixed with the dross of self-seeking or pride. Nonetheless, this is better than a total refusal and gives God a distinct opportunity to refine the motivation. If that refining process is sustained, the confirmation of the call will invariably be established.

We have already touched considerably on the perplexity that many, youths especially, experience over the call of God to special service. Even as we have shown that God treats us all uniquely as individuals in our call, so God gives a personalized confirmation in answer to our search and inquiry for an assurance of that call. Sooner or later, suddenly or slowly, silently or loudly, God will speak the word of conviction. Then will come the glorious certainty, and there's nothing like it.

We envy those who hear the call of God as clearly as a human voice. For most of us, the drama is absent. In lieu of this, God moves into our understanding and guides our judgment as these become informed by an increasing knowledge of His Holy Word. His call is as His breath upon our spirit, and our spirit in turn feels, understands, knows, and responds. It is the still, small voice of the Friend close by. His mind is read and His counsels are recognized by an intuition wrought by the Holy Spirit. This becomes confirmation enough, and a blinding flash of glory is not needed. Accompanying this calm assurance is a glorious certainty.

Every Christian *should know,* every Christian *may know* that he is in the place God wants him to be, doing the work God gave him to do. *That conviction, that certainty,* is for the doctor, the businessman, the professor, the housewife, the secretary, the minister, no less than the missionary. While the service of God is a special service and the call to it may have special features, yet the will of God, and therefore His call, covers all honorable occupations and all areas of a Christian's life. And since the command of Christ is already to go, the one who stays, even more than the one who goes, should want that special impression of the voice of God to him —that personal call—that God has promised.

You can know a conviction as a distinct feeling, after a time. Some of the tests are these: a conviction is permanent, a spring not a puddle; conviction is settled and constant, a tide not a wave; a conviction is specific and directed, a river not a swamp; and a conviction is confirmed not isolated . . .[1]

As suggested earlier, there may be a delay in this divine assurance. Among other reasons for this is that God may seek to test us for various purposes. His objective may be to break down our pride or, conversely, to bolster us against our feeling of inadequacy and unworthiness, but all in all, to teach us total reliance on Him. One prelate astutely put it this way, "The threefold requisite for an effective ministry is humility, humility, humility." God values this in His chosen servants.

There are several *possible* ways in which God may confirm a call to special service. We will enumerate a few of the best known. Additionally there are at least two *positive* methods He uses. These, too, will be mentioned subsequently.

POSSIBLE CONFIRMATION

Putting out the fleece.

The fact that the call may come by a mystical method does not necessarily carry with it a definite sense of confirmation. Gideon's experience proves this. Though an angel addressed him, he had his doubts, which led to the coining of the common phrase "putting out the fleece." This writer must admit that he has personally tried this but without satisfying results. However, this is not to question its validity, as we shall illustrate. It is mentioned to point out that it is not—or at least *may not be—for everyone*. It has worked for *some*.

The young preacher, Joseph Walker, was that evening in a particularly earnest mood. Unknown to anyone in

1. Taken from *Called of God—and Sure of It* by T. Norton Sterrett. © 1949 by Inter-Varsity Christian Fellowship and used by permission of Inter-Varsity Press. Italics added.

the building, he had asked for a sign from the Lord. He was at his own crossroads. Should he continue in his secular occupation and give all he could to the service of Christ as a local preacher? Or should he apply for full-time ministry?

He had decided that the ten-day mission he had been invited to conduct at Raymond Terrace was to provide the answer. If souls were converted under his preaching, he would offer all his life to the Methodist cause.

The decision was, in one way, out of his hands. He was only the mouthpiece of God. But if zeal and study and prayer could turn the scale by bringing in lost sheep, then he would be doubly sure.

Happy Joseph Walker! His calling was being confirmed. That night there were seven converts.[2]

Choosing lots.

This method appears in biblical form in several instances, one being the selection of a replacement for Judas as one of the twelve disciples (Acts 1:23–26). For those involved it was sufficient confirmation. It should be noted that such action was spiritually based:

> And they prayed, and said, Thou, Lord, who knowest the hearts of all men, show which one of these two Thou hast chosen to occupy this ministry and apostleship from which Judas turned aside to go to his own place. And they drew lots (Acts 1:24, 25) (NASB).

Although this method is not generally practiced and may be frowned upon as having much of the human element inherent in it, it does have its place. When leaders select followers for certain appointments after prayer and serious contemplation, is this not a form of choosing lots? Was this

2. Gilliard, Alfred J.: *All My Days.* London: Salvationist Publishing, pp. 21-22.

not what prevailed in the selection of Stephen and his six co-workers? Does this not eventuate into what may have been termed, "Called of God by appointment"? If the interplay of human judgment and error seems too prominent in such circumstances, cannot the persons involved rest comfortably in the assurance that man cannot put you where God cannot use you—if you are *available?* Consider, again Stephen!

Open doors.

One strong assurance of God's call for many has been the tremendous avenues of service that have been made available, once the individual has embarked on following the call of God. Doors that seem closed have opened. Obstacles and hindrances that seemed insurmountable have been removed. Paths that seemed dark have been flooded with light. This type of confirmation has close kinship to the circumstantial call and has been illustrated extensively in other chapters.

A word of caution! God, for His own reasons, has not always opened doors for some, asking only for blind faith. (Remember Abraham and Joseph?) Only afterward was the reason made known, and then not always to the individual being called.

Providential provisions.

Whom God calls He equips! Certainly He did not call Moses or Gideon or even Saul because they were fully equipped. In fact, at least two pleaded inadequacy. God's first requisite is a willing spirit, the abdication of self from the throne and the exaltation of Christ as Lord. This involves *not* the surrender of freedom (as is so commonly supposed) but the surrender of free will. Only then can He truly use whom He calls. Once this is done, it is no less than miraculous how He makes up, and helps *us* to make up, for our inadequacies. It is strange how a reluctance to answer the call to special service out of sheer inability to perform can be turned into a determination to catch opportunity as it comes, until preaching, or teaching, or whatever, becomes a compelling urge.

If God gives a man the call to preach in the sense of declaring His Word in the context of the ordained ministry, *He has His own ways of bringing this about* regardless of the blunders of the man concerned and the resulting blocking tactics of bureaucracy. That is how I came to be vicar of a parish of twenty thousand people in Dagenham.

The call to preach in the context of the ordained ministry came to me when my prejudices were against it, when academic qualifications and ecclesiastical circumstances were not in favour of my answering it, and the finance was beyond me. I am bound to say that the very snags which seemed to make it extremely unlikely, if not impossible, for me to answer that call have proved to be evidence that the call was God's and so He brought about the answer.[3]

A fruitful ministry.

"By this is My Father glorified, that you bear much fruit, and so prove to be My disciples" (Jn. 5:18) (NASB).

To many, the fulfillment of these words of Jesus is strong affirmation of the call and will of God. Not all will be privileged to reap an abundant harvest. There are those times when sowing, watering, nurturing, and cultivating will be the lot of some, while the harvest must be left to others.

Such was the life of the Scottish preacher who at the annual meeting, with downcast eyes, reported, "There was only one convert, the wee Bobby Moffat." In years to come Robert Moffat became known as the greatest among missionaries and had the adulation of royalty.

3. Joyce, C.A., editor: *My Call to the Ministry*. London: Marshall, Morgan & Scott, 1968, pp. 124-125. Used by permission. Italics added.

The fruit, however, be it great or little, will not only be a reward but to many, a strong confirmation to the faithful respondent to God's call. We recall the words of Jesus, "Joy shall be in heaven over *one* sinner that repenteth" (Luke 15:7).

It is interesting to note what Paul has to say about this. Following a rhetorical question, he unequivocally claims that the fruit of his labors is the endorsement of his authority and confirmation of his calling.

Are we starting to commend ourselves again? Or we do not, as some (false teachers), need written credentials or letters of recommendation to you or from you, (do we)?

(No, you) *yourselves are our letter of recommendation* (our credentials), written in your heart, to be (perceived, recognized,) known and read by everybody.

You show *and* make obvious that you are a letter from Christ delivered by us, not written with ink but with (the) Spirit of (the) living God, not on tablets of stone but on tablets of human hearts.

Such is the reliance and confidence that we have through Christ toward and with reference to God.

Not that we are fit (qualified and sufficient in ability) of ourselves to form personal judgments *or* to claim *or* count anything as coming from us; but our power *and* ability *and* sufficiency are from God.

(It is He) Who has qualified us (making us to be fit and worthy and sufficient) as ministers *and* dispensers of a new covenant (of salvation through Christ), not (ministers) of the letter—that is, of legally written code —but of the Spirit; for the code (of the Law) kills, but the (Holy) Spirit makes alive (2 Cor. 3:1–6) (AB).*

* Italics added.

POSITIVE CONFIRMATION

Although these are good weathervanes that may indicate and confirm the direction God has chosen for those whom He calls, there yet remain two positive experiences that will indubitably attend and undergird the obedient servant of God, whatever the nature of his calling. The aforementioned may not confirm the call for everyone. The two here mentioned will positively come to everyone as confirmation of their call to special service.

The peace of God.

The norm for every child of God who walks by faith in the direction God seems to lead is the experience of a sweet, settled peace. A basic reason for this is that God never *forces* us to move. He may put pressure on us to assist us in making the right decision, but the initial step must be our own. When we take that step, His sweet peace will be ours.

In contrast, Satan drives us against our best judgment, and even our will, into indiscreet action, if we allow our own self-will to predominate. Inevitably, there can only be soul upheaval and distress.

Typical of this is the native, veteran leader of India, Joseph Dahya. Experiencing a tremendous tumult of soul while resisting the call of God he climactically testified, "I went home that night and, at my bedside, made a complete surrender to God. Immediately *great peace flooded my being.*" Such also was the experience of a young minister now on the field:

I fought this calling for eight long years—I just couldn't do it! What would people think? I was a little too proud. Couldn't I serve the Lord just as well by working at home? *The inward fight was hard;* I was unhappy. The "Hound of Heaven" kept calling. I heard Him calling day and night. . . . At last I fell on my knees and said,

"All right, Lord." Oh, such joy and peace! God's way is *sure* of my calling.

Another descriptive account comes from the pen of C. Leslie Mitton:

> . . . in spite of all reasons in favour of the *status quo,* as the weeks went by I could not escape a growing awareness that the ministry probably was God's will for me. The inner discomfort of indecision and uncertainty became exceedingly distressing . . . It seemed that the time had come when some decision must be taken in order to relax the tension. To the question: Was God really requiring of me to offer for the ministry? The answer must in all honesty be "Yes." Otherwise, how explain the inescapable pressures of recent weeks to a course of action which, humanly speaking, seemed beset with difficulties and embarrassment? The next question was: Am I willing to do as God directs? It would have been a terrible betrayal of all I had derived from home and childhood to answer "no" to such a question. So with deliberation and finality I gave my answer: "Yes."
>
> I well remember the *sense of relief, gladness* and *inner freedom* which followed this clear-cut decision, . . .[4]

This peace can be disturbed by later decisions, conscious or unconscious. But, as long as we strive to do "what pleases Him," we will enjoy what Samuel Brengle described as either the *low tide* of a sanctified experience, which is "the peace of God which passeth all understanding," or the *high tide,* "joy unspeakable and full of glory."

The source of this peace is succinctly summed up by Lyell Rader, Sr., "Basically, it boils down to this, it is not so much a matter of whether or not God's voice is sufficently

4. Joyce, *op. cit.,* p. 77. Italics added.

clear so that we can be sure; rather it is a matter of whether or not we are sufficiently willing to mind God and trust Him implicitly." [5] This trust is personified in the childlike bedside prayer of the little girl who said, "We sure had a good time today, Lord. What have you got planned for tomorrow?"

The anointing of the Holy Spirit.

The Scriptures are filled with instances of the anointing of the Holy Spirit in reference to God's call of men and women to special service. A phrase commonly used to introduce this anointing is "The Spirit of the Lord came upon . . ." and then are listed in the Old Testament such persons as the seventy elders (Num. 11:35), Othniel (Judg. 3:10), Gideon (Judg. 6:34), Samson (Judg. 14:6), Saul (1 Sam. 10:10), David (1 Sam. 16:13), the messengers of Saul (1 Sam. 19:26), and a host of others. To each came a unique type of service such as prophesying, judging, or delivering.

In the New Testament, the messianic prophesy of Isaiah

> The Spirit of the Lord God is upon me because the Lord has anointed and qualified me to preach the gospel . . . (Isa. 61:1).

was read by Jesus (Luke 4:18) at the outset of his earthly ministry. Then, without qualification or veiled presumption He rightfully claimed, "This day is this Scripture fulfilled in your ears" (Luke 4:21). The foundation for His claim is related in Matthew's Gospel (3:16) when the Holy Spirit descended upon Jesus at His baptism by John.

Later Jesus testified, "He who sent me is ever with me; My Father has not left me alone, for I always do what pleases Him" (John 8:28) (AB).

Peter adds further confirmation by saying, "God anointed

5. Rader, Lyell, Sr.: *The War Cry.*

Him (Jesus of Nazareth) with the Holy Spirit . . . for God was with Him (Acts 10:38) (NASB).

This, with a host of experiences, brings us to the conclusion that whom God calls, He anoints and by this anointing *confirms* that calling.

> But as for you (the sacred appointment, the unction) the anointing which you received from Him abides (permanently) in you . . . (1 John 2:27) (AB).

It is *inconceivable* to think that a person could have the anointing of the Holy Spirit and not be aware of it! His presence is the *basic cause* for the peace mentioned earlier. It is one of the fruits of the Holy Spirit (Gal. 5:22, 23) and comes embryonically with that anointing.

The called of God who obey have much reason to rejoice over this anointing. This will be an absolute and inevitable confirmation of God's calling, ensuring His presence and powers in our own lives and reflected in the service to which He has called us—to the degree we are faithfully obedient. Paul exuberantly testifies to being made a minister,

> According to the gift of God's grace which was given to me according to the working of His power.
> To me, the very least of all saints this grace was given to preach to the Gentiles the unfathomable riches of Christ (Eph. 3:7, 8) (NASB).

At the beginning of this particular chapter Paul speaks of the stewardship of God's grace entrusted to him; then of the revelation of insight into the mystery of Christ that had been revealed to those in other generations and finally "to His holy apostles and prophets by the Spirit." He concludes by claiming the *Holy Spirit's presence and revelation.* This is the privilege of all ministers, the climactic confirmation of the call of God.

13
THE COST—
THE CONSEQUENCE

"I can never be the vessel He originally planned. Second best will have to do." This was the plaintive remark of a talented young woman who foolishly chose to be unequally yoked in marriage rather than to fulfill her call to special service. The young man was a professing Christian, talented, handsome, and persuasive. The only thing wrong was that he was not totally dedicated to God. Nor did he fit into God's plans for the one who became his wife. The marriage itself did not succeed, and for the rest of her life, she carried this regret in her heart and mind, even though she subsequently gave God dedicated but limited service.

How typical of many others! Here is the statement of another who woefully cried, "I could kick myself for the wonderful opportunity for full-time service I lost. I have no one to blame but myself. When God called, I closed the door, and it will never be open again." Alas, as with hundreds and thousands of others—this was all too true.

In the chapter on "Stop! Look! and Listen!" we dealt with the negative approach to the call. The purpose of this chapter is to help the reader avoid the *results* of a negative response to the call.

A PRICE TO PAY

Let's face it—obeying God is not always easy. It was never meant to be.

Where in the Bible do you read that the ministry is a bed of roses?

Where in the Bible do you read that a big salary (one you may truly need) is part of the ministry? And, does the Bible indicate that if you stopped preaching to get that salary, it would be all right?

Where in the Bible do you read that, as an evangelist, teacher, or missionary, you would be respected and well spoken of by all men?

Contrary to all this, Jesus promised only a cross to His followers, which included persecution, being despised, being hated (John 15:19), suffering, and even hunger. For some this means misunderstanding and loneliness; for others, especially women—the chance of remaining single rather than marrying.

Dr. Dick Hillis has pointed out that as a minister, God expects him to wear at least two hats. He is a soldier sliding on his belly into enemy territory, cutting the barbed wires of superstition to set the captives of Satan free. Then he is also a shepherd, feeding and protecting those he has freed.

Neither of these, he continues, is easy, but being a shepherd is the more exacting and fatiguing. After enumerating many of the demands on a shepherd whose sheep try his patience and drain his well dry, Hillis concludes with his own testimony:

Years ago in a little room in Los Angeles I listed those heavy demands and then right beside them placed only a sketchy record of what God has done for me. "God made Christ who did not know sin to be sin for me to make me God's righteousness in Him." I was suddenly overwhelmed by all Christ had done for me. His demands became so right, so reasonable, and so small when I compared them with the price He paid for me that I dropped on my knees and promised to follow Him.

Following has cost what Jesus said it would. But if once again I could be young and stand at that crossroad of serving self or serving Christ, I would without hesitation choose to serve Christ in the ministry, and thank Him every day for the privilege of doing so.[1]

1. Hillis, Dick: "The Challenge of the Ministry." *Christianity Today.*

For John Soong, a brilliant young Chinese student who obtained his Ph.D. in chemistry at Columbia University and whose future held great promise, the price was the same. Obviously, as a dedicated Christian, his calling appeared to be centered around his natural talents. But God had other plans. On the way back to China, John Soong tore up his degree and dropped it into the ocean. He went on to become China's greatest evangelist. Yes, he had a tremendous mind for science, but God had given him the spiritual gift of evangelism, and it was to this task that God wished him to devote his efforts.

Settle it, once and for all, obedience to God and His will involves a surrender of freedom, so-called. As Carl Lundquist strongly phrased it, this calls for a "radical obedience to Christ."

DON'T BLOW IT

As an administrative Youth Secretary, the author had the responsibility to plan and organize statewide youth conferences and rallies. On different occasions, in order to present the challenge to youth to dedicate their lives to special service, I called upon already dedicated young people to address their peers on the subjects of "I hear the Call—I will obey" and "I heard the Call, I am obeying."

One year, under the inspiration of the Holy Spirit, I felt led to ask a faithful lay leader of advanced years to follow these talks with a third subject "I heard the Call—I disobeyed." I knew the background of this individual and recognized this to be a delicate undertaking. Accepting this as a unique opportunity, this individual reviewed the call he had received in his youth and the negative choice he had made. He continued by describing his present service for God, his prosperous position in the business world, his satisfying home life, and material blessings. He climaxed all this by saying, "I should be happy, but I'm not!" Then with deep visible emotion he admitted nursing a lifelong regret at disobeying the call of God and concluded by urging his youthful listeners not to make the same error he had made. The effect upon the youths was most fruitful.

Alfred J. Gilliard in dealing with the subject of what happens if you refuse to answer God's call stated:

> God does not lose His temper with us and punish us as would an angry human being whose invitation to work for him had been spurned. His ways are not our ways.
>
> Nor does He force us to obey Him. Liberty to become one of His spokesmen, or to refuse, is as real as liberty to accept or reject His salvation. Judas first had liberty to accept the invitation of Jesus to join Him as a disciple and then to betray His Master into the hands of His enemies.
>
> The high privilege of leaving all to follow Him can be set aside just as we frequently set aside opportunities to improve our minds or develop our physical powers. And the consequence is much the same. The older we get, the more conscious we become of our foolishness in refusing the call to devote our lives to the highest purposes. Success in other occupations is not denied us. The fruits of toil and trustworthiness are not withheld from men and

women if they choose to serve God in a way they desire rather than the way He desired. But the sense of maximum achievement, the "crown of life" which for Christian people is the knowledge that the years have been put to the best advantage is not given because it has not been earned. . . . You cannot escape the universal human longing to be the best. You marry the best [person]. You want for your child "only the best." If you buy a car, you seek the best you can afford. If God puts into your heart a conviction that you should give your whole life to the work of building the Kingdom of God upon earth and you choose another way, you cannot avoid final regret at your second best choice.

How do you know this happens?

Here you must depend upon the witness of your elders. If they have turned defiant, have lost their vision and silenced the voice of conscience—and this is quite possible with any of us—they will declare that they are glad they took the road they have followed. If they have remained humble and faithful to the many opportunities remaining to them, they will speak of God's goodness and mercy attending them all the days of their life and then add, with a sad, apologetic smile, "But I should have been a minister."

Those few words cover a *continuing regret* they would like you to avoid.[2]

SECOND CHANCE

Does God ever give a second chance? If we reject the divine command, will He ever trust us again? In refusing His will and His way, will the great privilege be lost to us forever?

2. Gilliard, Alfred J.: "What Happens to You If You Refuse to Answer God's Call?" *The War Cry.*

Not always! The "Hound of Heaven" consistently calls and calls and calls *until* and *unless* we deliberately make spiritual shipwrecks of ourselves. And even then, to some, the disturbing call of God comes yet again and gives one last opportunity.

Jonah is probably the most eloquent testimony to this! After his deliberate attempt to escape God's plan, God stopped Jonah, exposed his guilt, chastised him, broke down his opposition, and sent him on his way to fulfill His plan. Likewise, He rebuked Balaam by an ass, David by a parable, Peter by a look. A modern-day counterpart is found in this candidate's application form for the ministry:

Christ called me when I was fourteen, at a Youth Conference. I heard the call and I answered, "Lord, send me." He called me not only to be a minister but also to make supreme sacrifices and go to the mission field. Thus, began my Christian experience and preparation for full-time service.

But it was I, not God, who directed my life. I went on to college and my Christian life suffered. The years of service and a positive Christian life quickly dissolved. I vacillated between sin and the world to occasional repentance. There followed many years of continuous attempts to lead a Christian life but yet hang on to the things of the world. The ministry was now out of sight, forever.

Now, as I look back over these nearly ten years, I am not pleased at what I did or was. I am sorrowful that I did not answer "the Call." God had plans for me that I willfully ignored. These years of uselessness, unhappiness, cannot be relived. . . . My college education and the musical talents that God has so generously given me must again be offered, in complete surrender, and I must take steps to seek out what God would have me do for Him.

I feel that it must be full-time service, somewhere, somehow. Only He knows what and where, but I must give up self and seek out His will, His work for my life.

Because God gave a second chance, this person is now joyfully serving Him in special service.

QUALIFIED COMMITMENT IS QUALIFIED FAVOR

But let none presume on God's patience or tempt providence. There is *no guarantee* that everyone who disobeys will continue to find the door open. Sufficient illustrations have already been cited to act as strong warnings. God still expects complete and total obedience, and his best rewards are for those who bow quickly and wholeheartedly to His will.

Engaging in a frenzy of activities in God's work, laudable and meritorious as it may seem, is not enough. God demands and expects total obedience.

Those who hesitate to give this to God at the outset, lose something en route. Barak in being called to deliver Israel lost the honor of the victory to a woman, Jael's wife, because he cringed at the call to responsibility. Incidentally, here is another excellent example of an *indirect call* of a *circumstantial nature*. It came from Deborah, who "said to him, Behold the Lord the God of Israel has commanded, Go and March . . ." (Judg. 4:6) (NASB).

Even Moses paid dearly for his hesitancy, brief though it was. In having Aaron as his spokesman because he felt inadequate to speak, he later suffered from the rebellion of his brother and sister, Miriam. Nor are we to overlook his trouble when Aaron led Israel into idolatry by the molding of the golden calf. This may not have happened if Aaron had not become a crutch for Moses' faltering obedience.

PARDON THE INTERRUPTION

Some of these incidents have to do with mismarriages. We break into the general flow of this chapter to speak to this all-too-common problem in answering and fulfilling the call to special service.

We are reminded of the strong admonition "Do not be unequally yoked up with unbelievers—do not make mismated alliances with them or come under a different yoke with them (inconsistent with your faith)" (2 Cor. 6:14) (AB). Such an alliance all too often negates the possibility to do special service for God. There are exceptions such as that typified by Hosea in the Old Testament. But this is rare and even here God uniquely allowed this situation to allegorically teach Israel a lesson of love and mercy.

The situation where an individual receives a call and is already with a mate who does not share the same call may be a serious one. This can create severe problems. This is especially true if the uncalled is reluctant to share the lot of the life-partner. However, if the call has come after marriage, more than likely God will present His call, sooner or later, to the one yet untouched. A simple illustration is furnished by a young couple now in the ministry, as related by the wife:

It came to a climax while [we were] repairing the bedroom ceiling. We were having a hard time getting the piece of material up. So we just quit. We were thinking of buying a piece of farm land and were to let the man know if we wanted it or not. It seemed we couldn't make up our minds. My husband asked me what I thought about getting the land. I told him that we may as well get it and hope that one of our children went into the ministry. Then he wanted to know if that was what I really wanted. I just began to cry. He told me that he had decided not to get the land because he felt he had been called to become a minister. Then we both started to cry. I told him that I had been called and prayed that God would show me what to do. I didn't want my husband to go to Bible school unless he was called. I was afraid if I told him I had been called, he might just think he was too, for we are very close to each other. God did help us, and we made up our minds then and there to follow God's call.

It must again be recognized that that call may not always be the same for each—most likely it will not. The matter of obedience must, of course, prevail with both. To the objection "But I'm not called like he or she is" must come the answer already presented: *every* Christian is called to general service. If God has called a life-partner to special service, to hinder that one is to deliberately oppose the will and the call of God, at least by association.

The greater tragedy is for the individual who has received a call to deliberately (and foolishly) take on a life-partner who is not one in spirit *before* the marriage. Only prayer and perseverance and the power of the Holy Spirit can help. Even then—none of these will violate the free will of the undedicated individual, and the situation may yet end in disaster. So much for that, but let it be a warning!

NEW ORDERS

What happens if God seems to lead or call in another direction? What if pressing family circumstances or physical weakness compel one to leave the strenuous life of his calling?

The imperative of wholehearted obedience must prevail! It is no shame to have to take a lighter burden if the motive is loyal to God's calling. They who find it necessary to change their form of service must take their calling with them as they remake their careers. The spirit of their commission must never leave them. No one can ever measure the contribution of those who were compelled to return to the area of general service. In God's plan, they may well have accomplished His objective. Refer back to the chapter on "Short-term service." In the final analysis, whatever the circumstances, the crucial test to those leaving the ministry is whether by doing so they are increasing their commitment to God or lessening it.

A change of course could be in the plan of God. Such was the experience of Philip leaving a burning revival in bustling Jerusalem to go to sit in the desert of Gaza until he met the Ethiopian eunuch. Paul's change of course from Asia Minor to Europe has already been noted. Little did either one realize at the time—or ever in life for that matter —that their obedience made them the instrument of carrying the gospel message to a whole new continent. Unquestioning obedience to God's call must never diminish.

A young minister speaking to a military general who had vast experience and knowledge of the work of missionaries in the British Empire in its heyday said, "Sir, don't you think it is a waste of time, energy, and manpower to send missionaries to heathen lands when the results are so little and there is equally great need right here in the homeland?"

The General looked him square in the eyes and sternly replied, "Young man! What are your orders?"

In the words of the great classic,

> Theirs not to reason why
> Theirs but to do or die.

WARNING!

But what about those who go back on their call? What are the consequences for them? As has already been pointed out in this chapter, it is more tragic, in some ways, than if they had never heeded the call to begin with. They always regret it. Billy Graham, who has had three presidents offer him top positions has, like many others before him, faced and settled this. He has said, "God has called me to preach, and I would never defer from that because my lips would turn to clay if I ever left what God has called me to do for something else." Much has already been said about this but a final word of warning must be given. Better suffer doing the thing God calls us to do than find comfort or escape in doing that which is outside His will. Better fail at working out the inner compulsions of the heart than to be a miserable success at what we know we are not called to do. The haunting, nagging, discomforting feeling of being a quitter, a runaway, a failure to God, will eat at the soul like the gnawing of a mouse or the dripping of a faucet in the quiet of the night. It has truly been said that we may choose the course of our calling but we can never choose the consequences of our choosing.

On the other hand, "the peace of God that passeth all understanding" is the lot of the obedient. The possession of this tranquility is the envy of the wealthy, the learned, the mighty and, most of all, of those who had it but lost it—a heavy price to pay!

> How willing is the man to go
>   Whom God hath never sent;
> How feeble, impotent and slow
>   The chosen instrument.

14

RECRUITING— YES OR NO?

It is a common practice among many denominations and groups to hold youth gatherings at which time the claims of Christ to salvation and sanctification are urged. Some go to the extent of making strong, specific appeals to special service as ministers and missionaries. At times, such appeals have come under severe criticism.

RIGHT OR WRONG?

One of the reasons for criticism is that the appeal to the emotions is excessively strong. Critics point out as evidence that many make commitments under such pressures and then later fall by the wayside before they enter into the ministry or while they are engaged in this pursuit. Although this may contain some truth, it has ever been so.

We will dispense with any lengthy debate over this argument by mentioning the experience of Jesus. Many followers enthusiastically indicated their desire and intention to be His disciples. After He outlined the sacrifices and hardships this would involve, the majority lost their enthusiasm and zeal and ceased following Jesus so that He turned to the original twelve and asked (one can imagine with pathos and sadness), "Will ye also leave me?"

Nevertheless, this type of appeal poses the question, "Is it wrong to recruit young people for special service?" The answer is *yes,* if it is merely a *human* effort.

This positive answer should have the added qualification that recruiting is wrong if it is done willy-nilly and without the direction of the Holy Spirit. There are those sincere but misdirected and overzealous souls (more prevalent in some circles than others) who feel that every person is a candidate for special service and should be pressed into the ministry. Not so!

While it is incumbent on every child of God to witness and serve Him in whatever sphere he may be in, only God, through the Holy Spirit, knows whom He wants, and when and where, for special service. Actually there are times when a pastor or leader should discourage individuals from entering into church-related occupations. A misdirected zeal is never a substitute for a call. To push beyond God's leading is to force an issue that results in the type of incident told about a particular farm boy who was unduly urged to enter the ministry. He felt no inclination or leading in this direction. One day, while plowing his fields, he saw a cloud formation in the sky that appeared to spell the letters *PC.* Because of the pressure he had been undergoing, he interpreted the letters to mean "Preach Christ" and immediately took steps to enter the ministry. Experience and time soon proved the lack of divine leading and success in this occupation. Eventually, in good conscience and judgment, he concluded that the better interpretation of *PC* was to "plant corn," which in his case was more accurate.

There are those who have been pushed into special service minus the leading or will of God. Let no one use this fact as an excuse to avoid such service. But neither let anyone presume to do the work of the Holy Spirit and try to fit people into molds of his own imagination.

HOWEVER, "THE LORD SAID..."

On the other hand, there is much in Scripture to lead and guide us in this matter. There are definite instances where God explicitly and directly instructed His servants to relay to others His call and command for special service. Mention has been made in earlier chapters of Aaron, the Levites, and Joshua. Various prophets serving as God's voice to Saul, David, Barak are further illustrations, typical of many others.

One other outstanding example deserves mention; that of Elijah to Elisha, as one prophet to another. The casting of the mantle by the former on the latter (1 Kings 19:19–21) was the only sign of the call, but it was enough. However, this came about only after instructions directly from God who said to Elijah, "Elisha . . . shalt thou anoint to be prophet in thy room" (1 Kings 19:16). These illustrations of the obvious direction of God as the *direct command* of God need no explanation.

THE GREAT COMMISSION—PART 2

But back to the original question. The answer is also "No! It is not wrong to recruit." In fact, it is wrong *not* to recruit. This seeming contradiction is, to use a common metaphor, the other side of the coin. There are not only, in the Bible, *direct* commands of God to specific individuals to approach another particular person, but there are also *indirect* commands of God for all to engage in recruitment.

The word "indirect" is carefully and cautiously used, for if we are to be governed, and properly so, by the laws of hermeneutics (the science of biblical interpretation) then the Great Commission, correctly understood, was given directly and only to the apostles. In part this is true, even though we tend to speak of it as being aimed at disciples of all generations.

We are inclined to place great stress on the first part of

this Great Commission—*Go, reach, teach,* and *win* souls, or "Go and make disciples." Well and good! However, in our strong emphasis on this first part, we fail to give the same strength to the equally important second part of this command, "Teaching them to *observe everything* that I have commanded you." The words "them" and "observe everything" allow for no exceptions. "Them" encompasses all disciples then, now, and forever, and places on each one, indirectly at least, the obligation to subsequently "Go and make disciples."

In this, as in all service for God, we must be sensitive to the person, presence, and leading of the Holy Spirit. In fact, the greatest service we can do in recruiting for the ministry, in addition to intense prayer, is to teach and lead potential candidates also to know, to be aware of and to become sensitive to the Holy Spirit.

Again, every command Jesus gave to the disciples is to be taught and becomes, indirectly, a command for all succeeding disciples.

Consequently, the command of Jesus to "pray the Lord of harvest to force out and thrust laborers into the harvest" (Matt. 9:38) (AB) becomes incumbent on all of us. Admittedly, this particular verse calls only for prayer on our part, but this means of communication is always a two-way conversation. As we speak to God, He will also speak to us and, in turn, will lead us to speak a word both in season and out of season that will influence someone to go to the harvest field. That's how it happened in the life of William Harris:

His call . . . came while [he was] serving with the R.A.F. in World War I. He promised God that if he came through, he would try to make his life count as an officer in the Salvation Army, and so it was. . . .

All this came out of a Sunday morning meeting in Brighton Congress Hall (church). Candidate Harris, playing in the band, was taking the programme for granted. Then "out of the blue" the treasurer, a dignified, conservative and a greatly respected business man, *declared himself strangely moved of God* to pass on a message for someone in the meeting. He then repeated Mark 16:15: "Go ye into all the world, and preach the gospel to every creature," and sat down.

In that dramatic moment God came to Harris and he was affected physically, mentally and spiritually. The message was for him. It was a firm call. He could not escape it.[1]

The call to special service is the work of the Holy Spirit, first, last, and always. If we are sensitive to Him, He will direct us when to speak and when to keep still, but always to "pray the Lord of harvest."

. . . Young people are still being stirred by the opportunity for growth and service in our Movement, and we should see that they are constantly aware of the devoted service of officers and soldiers [laymen] throughout the world. Have we a "Heroes' Gallery" in our own hearts? This is something we should cultivate. . . . Then do we bring our heroes and heroines to the notice of our young people? . . . If we do, there will be some young folk who will emulate these heroes and hear God's call through them. This is an *indirect* method, but is much more effective than an abstract, if direct, invitation to officership.

Nevertheless, the *direct* call must be made. . . . The personal word is most effective. *The personal word comes from one God-directed heart to the heart of another.* . . . The officer, aware of the burning need and conscious that men and women God wants are often not those souls whose eyes are on the ends of the earth, but those

1. "This Man Harris." *Vanguard,* April, 1960. Italics added.

who, integrated within and with their fellows, are happily serving in the corps [church] and desiring nothing more than present duty, go with an Elijah call to a young Elisha at the plough, or to a David with an instrument, or to an Esther serving in university or office or hospital.[2]

DON'T HOLD BACK

In speaking specifically to the need for missionaries, Clarence B. Bass, relating to the intensiveness of the Great Commission, declared that *each* Christian must take it as an individual command! Each of us must go! "But, he went on to point out, we cannot all go—physically and literally. Age, physical resources, and other circumstances prevent many of us in this respect. However, this does not relieve us of the responsibility to 'go.' Each of us must discover our own way of going!" This obligation puts a constant burden on *all* of God's people. Bass outlines three ways open to fulfilling this command:

1. Some of us have to *go!* (physically)
2. Some of us have to *let go!* (mentally)
3. Some of us have to *help go!* (spiritually)

The first point needs no amplification.

In his second point, Bass specifically mentions the influence of parents and their responsibility. There are those who, burdened for the salvation of mankind (at home as well as abroad), practically pray their children into the ministry. Their whole demeanor, dedication, and concern over lost souls impress upon the hearts and minds of their children the desperate urgency of the great need. Typically, the writer recalls a number of parents who have had all five

2. Editorial: "The Men God Wants." *The Officer.* Italics added.

of their children enter the ministry. This influence is borne out in one candidate's application:

> As a teen, I was rather bitter toward the church because I saw my parents get small, seemingly insignificant appointments, while others who had been much less faithful received large appointments. I felt all along that God was calling me to the ministry, but I ignored it. I knew I would be unhappy if I was out of the will of God, but I also felt that I would be even more unhappy as a minister. *As I matured I realized that the appointments Dad received were always accepted as from God and that God blessed him in them.* I finally accepted the call. I now feel that the greatest rewards do not always come in large appointments.

Unfortunately, there are other parents who foolishly discourage or even prevent their children from responding to the call of God. Ironically, some of these parents are themselves in the ministry. Affected by the difficulties they have endured, they want "only the best" for their children. No sacrifices, hardships, or humiliation such as they suffered, or as they have observed in the lives of others, for their offspring! Rather, they covet for their children what they couldn't afford or enjoy—comfort, a good home, position, prestige, a lack of pressure and persecution. Caught in the lofty but totally erroneous concept of this philosophy, they fail to see that "things" fail to give the peace and security they purport to achieve for their progeny.

HELP TO GO

A word about Bass' third point. His stress was on undergirding those who are willing to be obedient. Although his reference was to financial support, there is an even greater asset if we are to help attract, influence, and recruit candidates for special service. It is that intangible quality termed "spirit." Annie Johnson Flint beautifully endorses this philosophy in her poem.

Pray—Give—Go

Three things the Master hath to do.
And we who serve Him here below,
And long to see His kingdom come
May *Pray* or *Give* or *Go.*

He needs them all—the Open Hand,
The Willing Feet, the Praying Heart,
To work together and to weave
A threefold cord that shall not part.

Nor shall the giver count his gift
As greater than the worker's deed
Nor he in turn his service boast
Above the prayers that voice the need.

Not all can Go; not all can Give
To speed the message on its way,
But young or old, or rich or poor,
Or strong or weak—we all can Pray.

Pray that the gold-filled hands may Give,
To arm the others for the fray;
That those who hear the call may Go
and Pray—that other hearts may Pray!

Recently a leader of an international organization was decrying the lack of candidates for the ministry. In the main, he blamed affluence as the deterring factor. This may be true to some degree, but not totally!

It is the writer's conviction, born out of years of direct relationship with them, that youth and young adults will accept the challenge to obey God's call when it is properly presented.

If affluence is so forceful, then why is it that we have had the many protest movements and demonstrations by youth against the so-called system and the establishment? Much of it is not so much their unwillingness to sacrifice as it is their protest against the phoniness, double standards and, especially, materialism of our present society. On the other hand, what compels so many to respond to the challenge of a service corps or VISTA at great personal sacrifice?

Don't call youth to sacrifice and service and expect them to respond if they witness leaders jockeying for position and promotion or seeking accommodations that smack of extravagance rather than self-sacrifice. One youth conclave representing a large denomination openly voiced their objection to conferences held in high-priced hotels where costly meals were part of the conference expense.

Youth is idealistic. If the challenge is clear and pure, most will respond. But the voice and hands that beckon must themselves be clean, self-sacrificing, and exemplify the ideal to which they call.

A case in point is the familiar story of the call of God to Samuel. It was said of this lad that "Samuel did not yet *know* the Lord" (Isa. 3:7) while he was serving in the temple under the influence of Eli. The old retiring priest was jealous for his distinguished office and reluctant to leave it to another. Although he had two sons who could have succeeded him, they were of unworthy character. God had to reveal to Eli that Samuel was the chosen vessel for the sacred duties pertaining to the temple. The interesting fact, easily overlooked, is that God's call to Samuel was actually revealed to Eli first. Only after He interpreted this call to Samuel, did the boy realize that it was the voice of God. Meanwhile, Eli was a pure channel used of God.

Today, as in biblical times, God most often chooses to

work through human instruments. It is our sacred privilege and obligation to be channels. It is equally incumbent on us to be clean channels. Dr. Henry Hitt Crane lists three practical but basic requisites for attracting recruits:

First: The minister (speaking of himself) must incarnate the principles he preaches. It is only the "word made flesh" that is deeply effective.

Second: The minister must deliberately and selectively proffer an invitation to enter the Christian ministry to the most promising young people he knows, not casually, with the conviction that he is paying them both his sincerest compliment and severest challenge.

Third: The minister must frankly give the prospective candidate a thoroughly realistic interpretation of the Christian ministry. He must point out that it is the easiest job in the world "to get by with" and the hardest job there is "to make good in." His descriptive analysis of the ministry and its demands are challenging:

> Really to be worthy of this vocation a man must strive terrifically to outwork and to outlove everyone in his acquaintance.
>
> Rightly conceived, it is the most exacting profession there is and the most exciting and emancipating. It is the most intimate, and the most public; the most strenuous, and the most satisfying; the most revealing, and the most rewarding.
>
> Its temptation is to become a conventional priest; its highest challenge, to become a prophet of God.

In the final analysis we reemphasize that the Holy Spirit is the power and motivating force that operates in and through these channels.

Wrote Catherine Booth to her eldest son, Bramwell: "Oh, my boy, the Lord wants such as you to go out among the people. . . . You are free to do it. Will you not rise to your destiny? You can preach and you ought to preach." God was using a mother to call her son of twenty years.

We conclude this chapter with a quotation from the intuitive pen of that son who was destined later to become the second general of the Salvation Army. What an example he had in his parents!

It is, then, amongst men and women thus united by a common love for Christ and for each other, and so influenced by a common desire for the salvation of the people around them, that we seek for those who are to become "fishers of men" *in a yet wider sense.* It is by many means that we find them. Every officer is urged constantly to be on the watch for them; our literature frequently contains appeals designed to influence them. Special meetings are held occasionally, at which we gather young people likely to prove of good service if they were willing to devote their lives to the work, when the subject is dealt with by suitable teachers.

But it is not to any of these means, at any rate so far as we can tell, *that we owe the large majority of the consecrated lives that are offered to us. It is rather to that direct and definite impulse,* born, I believe, *of the Spirit of God,* which is usually described by those who recognize it as "the *call to the work."* There is, I admit, sometimes an illusion. There is sometimes, perhaps, an element of selfish ambition. There is sometimes, possibly, a mere impression, passing away more quickly even than when it came. But in the majority of cases that call is a very real, a very beautiful, a very powerful, occasionally a very terrible, visitation, exercising an extraordinary influence over the lives of those who receive it, and often bringing about results, both immediate and remote, which altogether astonish those to whom they are known.[3]

3. Booth, Bramwell: *Servants of All.* The Salvation Army, 1899, pp. 26-29. Italics added.

15
HOW IT
HAPPENED TO ME

Throughout this book mention has been made of many persons and their calls, who served as examples of the various points that were being stressed. Purposely, these have been brief, lest the illustration overshadow the illustrated.

The whole of this chapter is to present notable persons who have shared their most intimate experience, the Call of God. The purpose is to exemplify further that, as in biblical and ancient times, God still calls. He has and uses many methods and in one way or another they all fit into the three types described in this book.

These stories will be presented as told by the individuals, either as direct quotations or transcribed by other writers. No comments or applications will be employed. They shall speak for themselves, and the readers will make their own applications. It is hoped that great inspiration, in addition to any received heretofore, will attend the readers and greater light will be their reward.

Keep one thing in mind. These were human beings, made of the same common clay as all of us. The essence of the

Call of God to special service includes four ingredients or steps:

1. A call must be *uttered,* which calls for the action of a *voice.*
2. A call must be *heard,* which calls for the action of an *ear.*
3. A call must be *responded to,* which calls for the action of a *heart.*
4. A call must be *obeyed,* which calls for the action of the *mind.*

In his will God takes care of the first. He can break the barrier of the second. The third and fourth steps are man's alone as they relate to his will and willingness. The consummation of God's call demands a wholehearted cooperation between the person and his God. If these persons recorded here achieved great distinction and were used mightily of God, it was not only God's choosing, it was their choosing—their willingness to be obedient—to be anything and everything He wanted.

Go thou and do likewise (Luke 10:37).

BILLY GRAHAM

On the third Sunday in May, 1940, twenty-one-year-old Billy Graham, ready for his graduation exercises from the Florida Bible Institute near Tampa, Florida, preached, as he regularly did, at a nearby trailer camp. Exactly fifteen years later, on the third Sunday in May, 1955, the British Court Calendar carried this announcement:

The Queen and the Duke of Edinburgh attended Divine Service this morning in the private Chapel, the Royal Lodge. Dr. William Graham preached the sermon.

. . . And though Windsor is separated, not in miles only, by a great distance from Tampa and though his pulpit manner before the royal family was considerably more subdued than anything his trailer-camp congregation was used to, it is safe to say that the quality which distinguished his preaching was the same in both places; he spoke "as one having authority."

To understand how he came by that preaching authority, it is necessary to go back to his preaching origins. These origins could hardly have been humbler, intellectually, or more conservative, theologically, or better calculated, spiritually, to produce the kind of preacher he is. The power he has today is rooted in those beginnings.

He was seventeen at his conversion, a senior at the Sharon, North Carolina, High School. His conversion did not result, for him in a blinding revelation that he was called to preach. He was, in fact, slow to make up his mind—not slow by what is ordinarily expected of a seventeen-year-old, but slow when one considers what extraordinary expectations were centered in him. He still had a lurking idea he might play baseball—whetted by the few semipro games he actually played at $10 to $15 a game. But during that summer he never was for long beyond the reach of influences which made it unlikely he would ever go in for so secular a pursuit and unlikely that he could forget that preaching might be, in the devout and weighted phrase, "God's will for him."

Chief among these influences was the prayerful solicitude of his parents. . . . [His father], a quiet, gentle man, was not given to pressuring or argument; his prayers at the family altar nonetheless left no doubt of the hope he held that his ambition would be realized in his son. . . .

Billy's mother, soon after his conversion, set aside a period every day for prayer devoted solely to Billy and the "calling" she believed was his. She continued those prayers, never missing a day, for seven years until the last uncertainty was resolved and Billy was well on his preaching way. . . .

Another influence turning Billy toward preaching was his friend, Grady Wilson, who had followed close behind that night in the revival tent of Mordecai Ham. Grady, almost at once, had made up his mind to preach. Moreover, he started right off preaching . . . But the fact that Grady knew what he was going to do with his life and was so sure that nothing of comparable importance with preaching could possibly be done with it, undoubtedly kept the issue alive and pressing in Billy's mind.

It was partly because of his meeting with three fervent Bob Jones students and partly because his parents "hoped" he would attend a Bible college that Billy in the fall of 1936 entered Bob Jones College in Cleveland, Tennessee. . . .

But he did not stay long at Bob Jones College. In his uncertain frame of mind he found the religious rigidity of the place oppressive. Dr. Jones was a difficult taskmaster. There were rules and regulations galore, a too regimented social life, no intercollegiate sports. Billy, unfamiliar with such restraints and unhappy about them, was involved in an escapade or two which—though he eloquently talked his way out of them—left him marked as a possible "problem." He left at the end of the first semester.

The school Billy moved to from Bob Jones College was the Florida Bible Institute at Temple Terrace, near Tampa, Florida, now called Trinity College and located at Clearwater, Florida. Billy's choice of the Florida Bible Institute may have been partly due to a long siege he had with the flu, partly due to his love of baseball and the lure of being near the training camps of several major-league teams. The likeliest explanation is that Wendell Phillips, his roommate at Bob Jones, had gone on ahead and sent back a stream of letters which were both evangelically and climatically aglow.

"I told him," says Phillips, "that his decision was a matter for serious prayer: that schools were not the primary things, but that knowing God's will was of the utmost importance.

In every letter I referred him to Proverbs 16:9: 'A man's heart deviseth his way; but the Lord directeth his steps.' "

Billy Graham is sure the Lord's directing hand was in his move to the Florida Bible Institute. It was there he made his decision to preach and there he began to lay hold of and, in practice, test the convictions which today give authority to his preaching.

By technical educational standards, it was not much of a school. . . . Head of the Florida Bible Institute was Dr. William T. Watson, minister of a Christian and Missionary Alliance Church in Tampa. Preachers did all the teaching— aided, now and then, by visiting ministers and evangelists. The doctrines of the school were Biblical fundamentalism . . .

Even the regard of the girl students for the boys generally involved religious considerations. . . .

[It was at this time that Billy was involved in a romance, which was intense but brief and ended when he was rejected for another.]

That, with the cosmic finality of undergraduate romance, "finished" Billy. To Wendell Phillips, home on sick leave, he wrote: "All the stars have fallen out of my sky. There is nothing to live for. We have broken up." Wendell was quick with consolation—framed, as one would expect, in a bracket which gave his words authority. "Read Romans 8:28," he wrote " 'And we know that all things work together for good to them that love God, to them who are the called according to His purpose . . .' "

For Billy, who had spent most of several previous nights walking off his "desolation" on a nearby golf course, that was a prescription he could accept and one he knew how to take. It worked—even beyond what Wendell Phillips had hoped. "I have settled it once and for all with the Lord." Billy wrote. "No girl or friend or anything shall ever come first in my life. I have resolved that the Lord Jesus Christ shall have all of me. I care not what the future holds. I have determined to follow Him at any cost."

Although this consequence of unrequited love was only one of many factors in the process of making up his mind to preach, there is no doubt that, thereafter, Billy acted as a young man headed for the ministry should act. He buckled down to his studies. Most of all, he buckled down to a class he was taking in practice preaching. Not content merely to outline a sermon and, then trusting the Lord for the right words for the right place, preaching it from notes, he took to writing his sermons in full and then reading them aloud.

Such rehearsing—even in a place so favorably inclined to all kinds of sermons at all kinds of hours—was not possible in the congested dormitory. Billy's courage was not up to trying out in the chapel. He found his spot in a remote corner of the campus: a stump, well-hidden by trees at the swampy edge of the Hillsboro River. There, hour after hour, he did his practicing. "If there were no kind words from the audience," he says, "neither was there any criticism." When he found a sermon in a book of sermons he copied that—with adaptations—and preached it. When visiting preachers came to the school, he took notes of their pulpit mannerisms and tried them out—gesture by gesture, oddity by oddity—from his stump. From these services—invocation to altar call to benediction—he omitted nothing.

"Many times, surrounded by darkness," he says, "I called out from that cypress stump and asked sinners to come forward and accept Christ. There were none to come, of course. But as I waited I seemed to hear a voice within me saying, 'One day there will be many.' "

This went on for several months; Billy, meanwhile increasing in preaching facility and discovering, also, that he liked it. After one such solitary sermon had ended with the usual unheard altar call, Billy suddenly found himself stirred by his own appeal. That night he walked the golf course again, "arguing with the Lord," sometimes out loud, against preaching: "I can't preach . . . I couldn't learn to preach . . . I don't want to preach . . . No church would have me."

"God," said Billy, "talked right back: 'I can use you . . . I need you . . . You make the choice, I will find the place . . .' "

Finally, past midnight, Billy said, "All right, Lord, if You want me, You've got me." Later that night he wrote a one-sentence letter to his parents: "Dear Mother and Dad: I feel that God has called me to be a preacher."

. . . When, in 1940, Billy graduated from the Florida Bible Institute, his religious faith was past the experimental stage; his commitment to what he believed to be God's will was unconditional; the Bible, from having been a book of reference, had become, for him, God's Word, and he was thoroughly at home in it; his preaching had many lacks, but —rooted in the Scriptures and his personal experiences— a note of authority was not one of them." [1]

SAMUEL LOGAN BRENGLE

. . . Another friend and fraternity brother was a nervous, ambitious youth who had signed himself Albert Jeremiah Beveridge. Popular and friendly with all, there was none with whom he was more fraternal than Brengle. They had a great deal in common, these two. Both had become widely known; both were almost inordinately ambitious; both were looking forward to political careers.

Candor of thought and feeling on all subjects was a hallmark of their companionship. One day, in discussing religion, Brengle told how he had gone to the mourners' bench five times, and had experienced nothing; and how one night, when coming across the lonely prairie, a Witness at length had spoken to him, giving him evidence which, though perhaps it would not be allowed in courts, had satisfied all questionings in his soul, and forever silenced the "prosecuting attorney" within. That was language that embryonic lawyers could understand, and the result of this talk was

1. High, Stanley: *Billy Graham.* New York: McGraw-Hill Book Co., 1956, pp. 69-77. Used by permission.

that one night, at a revival meeting being held near the university, Brengle led Beveridge to the altar, and later to church membership.

Between classes these two strolled the campus together, talking of oratory, politics, their law ambitions. Perhaps, they confided, when both were graduated they would together practice law, together seek the prizes of statecraft, remain pals with one goal. Now and then, however, Brengle would shake the foundations of these air castles by telling Beveridge of the peculiar leanings and drawings toward the ministry, which he felt at times. Somehow, he would say, he could not get away from the haunting thought of his father having been called to preach, but having drawn back; of his parents having dedicated him to the ministry when he was only a babe; of the fact that now whenever he heard a preacher expounding the Word, it rang in his ears with almost irresistible appeal.

The days passed. Brengle was in his last term at the university. To this point in his life, the idea of preaching—"the Call"—had followed him, flitting across every horizon he created, intruding itself in the midst of his most roseate dreams, sounding like a distant echo in every valley of his vision.

Then in the fall of 1882 the Call stepped out of its obscurity, blocked his path, demanded a decision.

It happened in Providence, Rhode Island, where Delta Kappa Epsilon was having its annual convention. An important matter—one involving the very life of the DePauw chapter—had to be brought before the convention and Brengle, as the chosen delegate from his university, had come halfway across the country to attend. In order to solicit the support of other chapters, he had spent considerable time on the way, stopping off to visit many of the leading colleges between Greencastle and Providence.

He was met at his destination by the delegates from a chapter particularly opposed to his, who informed him flatly, "We will fight you to the death." Going to his room in the Narragansett Hotel, Brengle felt the weight of his mission. Never before, he told himself, had he undertaken a task so responsible. His own destiny, the destiny of his fraternity chapter, the very honor of his university, depended, he felt, upon his being able to carry the convention.

Heavily burdened and scarcely able to collect his thoughts for the attempt he had to make to save his chapter, he went out into the street, walked awhile, and then came back to his room where, exasperated by this inexplicable depression, he threw himself on his knees and besought God to help him win. He seemed, however, to gain nothing by the exercise; his soul was lonely, and within, all was dark as night. He rose, went out on the street again, returned, knelt again, prayed again. Still the loneliness, the depression, the darkness. Yet a third time he went out on the street, returned, prayed. While praying this time, the thought of preaching was suddenly presented to his mind. Considering the idea irrelevant, he sought impatiently to shake it off—but without success. A tremendous inner battle occupied the following minutes, but when at length he exclaimed aloud, "O Lord, if Thou wilt help me to win this case, I will preach!" The whole room seemed instantly to flame with light.

The next day, his soul bathed in a peculiarly comforting feeling, he went to the convention hall, delivered his speech from the floor, offered his motion, and to his intense surprise the very men who had sworn they would fight him "to the death" rose to support the motion that meant reinstatement and recognition for his chapter. His victory was sweeping and entire. Furthermore, after the session many crowded about him to say that if the convention had not already been organized that speech would have ensured his being elected its president.

Back at the university, he told Beveridge of his experience, winding up with: "So you see, Bev old boy, I've got to preach!" Beveridge, notwithstanding the evident force of his friend's conviction, did not prove tractable. For an hour he argued, reminded Brengle of their dreams and ambitions, created new visions of fascinating brilliance, and said again and again, "Sam, you'll be a fool to go into the ministry!"

But the die was cast. God had kept His part of the contract made in the Providence hotel. Brengle, too, would keep his.

The word got about the campus that Brengle had given up the idea of law and politics for the church and preaching. Some, like Beveridge, urged him not to be foolish; others, however, rejoiced in his decision and the stubbornness with which he held to it. . . .

The Salvation Army and Sam Brengle arrived at Boston almost simultaneously. Though the organization and the man were two streams, originating at far distant points of the earth, and, up to now, following courses widely divergent, the hand of God had written that they would converge, become one, and flow on together to the blessing of nations. And Boston was to be the point of convergence.

By reason of the fact that he led a more or less sequestered life at the seminary, pursuing his studies and seeking out the higher and deeper things of God, several months passed before Brengle had any personal contact with The Army. At length, however, dribblings of hearsay began to reach him. Reports in the papers, telling of The Army "opening fire upon Boston," caught his eye. Stories descriptive of the Salvationists' strange methods, peculiar dress, and exuberant zeal in the face of persecution, also attracted his attention. . . .

Hence, one day, when Briggs had the Army officers as their guests for a meal at the seminary, he seized the opportunity to meet them, sizing up in a flash their spiritual equipment, swapping experiences with them, and immediately feeling they were kindred spirits and that his and their motivations, ambitions, heaven-born passions, were kith and kin. Into his heart there crept the thought, though as yet only a whisper, "These are my people!"

Years afterward, sorting out his first impressions, he said:

Two or three things appealed to me when I first met the Army. One was their sacrificial spirit. Another was their virility. I shall never forget going down to the Number 1 Corps hall in Boston and seeing the officer in charge, Major Gay, come in blowing his trumpet, marching erect and with vigor, and preaching sermons with fire and bite in them. These Salvationists were so different from the theological students who were so soft and easy, so anaemic as compared with men like Gay.

With every contact, his interest in The Army waxed stronger. As a student pastor he had a church three miles from the seminary. On the way to his Sunday service, he had to pass the Army's Number 2 Corps, and soon acquired the habit of dropping in for the early morning "knee-drill." He was seen, too, at other meetings during the week. Copies of *The War Cry* fell into his hands; and when he went on the train, he would take a few of the papers with him, passing them out to strangers to read.

And the more his contacts, the more insistently the new thought creeping over his heart whispered, "These are my people!"

. . . In the fall of 1885 came William Booth, paying his first visit to America. A minor hall in Tremont Temple, Boston, was filled with preachers, several hundred strong, who had gathered to see and hear at first hand just what this General of the much-publicized Salvation Army was like. Brengle, as student pastor of one of the city churches, was seated with the others awaiting the entry of the General. . . .

Meanwhile, William Booth, with his virile address and

his quiet, comprehensive answers to questions—many of which Brengle felt were not asked in either the spirit of brotherly love or of honest inquiry—carried his critical audience by storm. When the meeting was over, Brengle moved up with others to shake the General's hand. Coming abreast of that flaming crest with its "Blood and Fire," he murmured a wistful "I wish I could join you." This the General either did not hear or did not take seriously, since he gave no reply other than a pressure of the hand.

That night the General conducted an "all night of prayer" in which, among others, one of Brengle's fellow students, Charles R. Brown (later dean of Divinity School, Yale University), was converted. Brengle attended and his allegiance to the General was still more securely cemented. The following day he was again touched by an address which Booth, at the invitation of Sam's chum, Hayes, gave to the students of the Theological Seminary.

After Booth had gone, days came when Brengle felt more and more the urgency of beginning at once upon his full-time ministry. The necessity for spending long hours probing the subtleties of theology, the casuistries of seminary classrooms, the adaptations and embroideries of dogma and creed, the application of science's light and scholarship's criticism to the whittled-down fine points of religion—these began to irk him.

In the midst of his urge to be up and doing there came a brilliant and tempting offer. Out in South Bend, Indiana, a man named Clement Studebaker, builder of vehicles and of a fortune that had soared into many millions, had recently built a beautiful church, claimed by South Benders to be the finest Methodist edifice in Northern Indiana. In casting about for a suitable pastor, Studebaker had appealed to Dr. Gobin, Vice-President of DePauw University, for a recommendation. Dr. Gobin had written by return mail: "Brengle is the man you want." A few days later Brengle was surprised by receiving three letters, one from Dr. Gobin, another from the district superintendent of the Methodist church, and a third from Studebaker himself, each asking him to accept the pastorate of the "Studebaker Church."

What an offer! Here was honor, here a way out of the debt into which he had had to plunge to come to Boston and the seminary, here a large wealthy congregation, here an immediate and instant leap over the poor appointments and small memberships and perplexities that have to be hurdled by the average preacher before reaching so desirable a goal. But he made no hasty decision. Better hold his answer in abeyance for a few days, he reasoned with himself, until he could return to earth, think clearly, pray intelligently.

Meanwhile, taking a recess from his studies to ponder the matter, he attended a holiness convention in Baltimore. Dr. G. D. Watson, whose books he had read with blessing, was the preacher, and the convention was under the general leadership of his friend Dr. William McDonald. Ten days he spent thus, reveling in the rich and searching expositions given by Watson.

On the Sunday morning, having been asked to preach in the oldest Methodist church in Baltimore—the Utah Street church—he conducted a service whose fruitful results did much to swing him toward the course God had laid out for him. It was at this period that Brengle felt a definite call to evangelistic work.

That it was a call, and not simply a home-grown impulse of his own desire, was evident by the way he received it: he was staggered at the thought, offered argument against it, to which the vision of the beautiful affluent Studebaker Church added force. Feeling, however, that the call was coming directly from God, he just as directly appealed his case to God: "Lord, I am $500 in debt for my education, and the people of New England where I am now living do not know me. If I go into evangelistic work, how can I go about the country preaching holiness with these debts unpaid? The people may not give me enough money to pay them."

On the one side: the Studebaker Church, with its big salary, its important place, its wide pulpit. On the other: evangelistic work, with its prospect of debts, uncertainty, itinerancy. How could he decide?

The Holy Spirit came to his aid. His mind was led to Jesus' words in the sixth chapter of Matthew: "Take no thought, saying What shall we eat? or, What shall we drink? or Wherewithal shall we be clothed? . . . your heavenly Father knoweth that ye have need of all these things. But seek ye first the Kingdom of God." The spirit then took him over into Exodus, where he was reminded how God had led out from under the iron hand of Pharaoh a million Israelites with their wives, children, herds, and fed them for forty years in the wilderness. Thus pliant to the Spirit's guiding, Brengle thought he heard God Himself whisper to his heart: "Can you not trust Me? If I could care for those Israelites in a desert land, cannot I supply all your needs in rich New England?"

The question was settled. Out came pen and paper, and soon a letter was on its way to Mr. Studebaker in South Bend; in this letter the Reverend S. L. Brengle declined with thanks the flattering offer of the pastorate of "the finest church in Northern Indiana."

. . . Returning with renewed zeal and confidence to his evangelistic work, he found his labors doubly blessed of God. . . .

There was, nonetheless, still another step he must take before he had reached the place for which God had been training him. Hints for his Lord's purpose for him came to Brengle at times, such as, for example, when he would pass a Salvation Army open-air meeting, or conduct a campaign in an Army hall, or associate in other ways with the uniform . . . bringing again and again that persistent whispering in his heart of the thought: "These are my people!"

The taking of that step was just ahead. . . .

In the meantime Brengle had given himself to other thoughts . . . Chief among these was the question of whether he would follow what he had for many months recognized as God's leading, and offer himself as a candidate for officership in The Salvation Army. This he met with characteristic thoroughness and expedition. . . .

On June 1, 1887, at The Army's International Headquarters in London, two men sat in an office, facing each other. Twinkling hazel eyes of Samuel Logan Brengle, twenty-seven, looked deep into piercing gray eyes of William Booth, fifty-eight.

"General, I have come." [2]

PETER MARSHALL

Peter Marshall did not grow up wanting to be a minister. That was God's idea—not his. In fact, it took quite a lot of divine persuasion to get him to accept that plan.

Peter's first adolescent ambition was to become a deck apprentice in the British Mercantile Marine and, of course, eventually rise to nothing less than an admiral. . . .

His navy "career" lasted but two days . . .

Peter did not understand it then, but this was the first big step in God's guidance for his life. Often God has to shut a door in our face, so that He can subsequently open the door through which He wants us to go. People today wonder about this matter of God having a detailed plan, a

2. Hall, Clarence: *Samuel Logan Brengle*. New York: The Salvation Army National Information Service, 1933, pp. 43-46, 62-64, 69-75, 77, 78, 83, 87. Used by permission.

blueprint, for each individual in the universe. "If there is really a God," they ask, "and if He is interested in *me*, how do I go about getting in touch with Him? *How* does He talk to people today?"

Peter Marshall's story answers these questions out of one man's rich experience. I can imagine God saying: "There is a boy down in Lanarkshire. I have a plan for him. He is to go to America, in order to enter the ministry. He will spend almost half his life in the United States. His life and his ministry will bless thousands of people. I have all the circumstances planned and all my helpers designated, to make sure that my plan does not go awry." So the hand that firmly shut the door to a career in the Royal Navy, in order to open the way into the ministry, was really God's—not man's. . . .

Although Peter was now approaching his twenty-first birthday, he was still restless and dissatisfied at home. Eventually the time arrived when he decided that it was best for him to leave the family circle and strike out for himself.

His mother was sympathetic and helpful. She had supplied a steadying hand throughout his uneasy childhood. . . .

When the trunk was all packed, she walked to the little iron gate with him. It was when her heart dictated affection, which a reserve, deep inside her, would not let her lips express, that she lapsed into the "braid Scots" of her childhood. It sprang naturally to her lips at this moment.

"Dinna forget your verse, my laddie," she said. "Seek ye first the kingdom of God and his righteousness, and all these things shall be added unto you" (Matthew 6:33). Her blue eyes smiled reassuringly at him. "Long ago I pit ye in the Lord's hands, and I'll no be takin' ye awa noo. He will tak' care o' you. Dinna worry."

. . . Another very strong influence on Peter during these most impressionable years was his intense admiration for Eric Liddell. Eric was Scotland's greatest and best-loved athlete, a divinity student who planned to be a missionary.

. . . In 1924 he was chosen to run in the Paris Olympics. But he electrified Britons by refusing unequivocally to run the 100 meter, when he discovered that the "heats" were to be run off on a Sunday. At great sacrifice, he decided to train for the 400 meter. . . .

Just before the start of the race, a band of Cameron Highlanders played in the stadium—always a blood-stirring experience for any Scotsman. As they finished, a man slipped up to Liddell and put a piece of paper in his hand. On it was written these words, "Them that honour me will I honour" (1 Samuel 2:30). Exactly 47.6 seconds later the unknown friend's prophecy was fulfilled. Eric had established a new world's record for the 400 meter and a reputation for the greatest quarter-miler yet seen.

Peter Marshall, along with thousands more young people in Scotland, followed every detail of all this. To them Eric was a hero, not just because of his great athletic ability, but also because of his modesty, his undeniable charm, the great strength of his Christian witness. His influence on Peter's life can scarcely be measured.

One summer Peter spent working in the English village of Bamburgh . . . Walking back from a nearby village to Bamburgh one dark, starless night, Peter struck out across the moors, thinking he would take a short cut. He knew that there was a deep deserted limestone quarry close by the Glororum Road, but he thought he could avoid that danger spot. The night was inky black, eerie. There was only the sound of the wind through the heather-stained moorland, the noisy clamor of wild muir fowl as his footsteps disturbed them, the occasional far-off bleating of a sheep.

Suddenly he heard someone call, *"Peter! . . ."* There was a great urgency in the voice.

He stopped. "Yes, who is it? What do you want?"

For a second he listened, but there was no response, only the sound of the wind. The moor seemed completely deserted.

Thinking he must have been mistaken, he walked on a few paces. Then he heard it again, even more urgently:

"Peter! . . ."

He stopped dead still, trying to peer into that impenetrable darkness, but suddenly stumbled and fell to his knees. Putting out his hands to catch himself, he found nothing there. As he cautiously investigated, feeling around in a semicircle, he found himself to be on the very brink of an abandoned stone quarry. Just one step more would have sent him plummeting into space to certain death.

This incident made an unforgettable impression on Peter. There was never any doubt in his mind about the source of that Voice. He felt that God must have some great purpose for his life, to have intervened so specifically. Through subsequent years there were other close brushes with death, times when he was spared, while others around him were hurt or killed. . . .

Out of his experiences during these years, Peter coined the phrase "God's nugatory influences." During this early part of his life, however, God's influences often seemed more determined than merely nugatory. God's next step in channeling his life toward the one goal of the ministry now became evident.

That fall, a missionary returned from China spoke to the young people in the Buchanan Street Kirk. He came as a representative of the London Missionary Society, and was not seeking money, but recruits—volunteers for life for the mission fields.

Peter was deeply touched by this appeal. . . . In addition, Eric Liddell had just announced that he was going to China as a missionary under the auspices of the Congregational Church. Peter longed to follow in his hero's steps.

At any rate, whatever the influences, from that moment, Peter knew that his call was for full-time Christian service. That afternoon, at the close of the meeting, he stood up and stated publicly that he accepted the missionary's challenge.

"I have determined," he said, "to give my life to God for Him to use me wherever He wants me."

As often happens, there was a sharp disillusionment in the contrast between the adventurous spirit in which he sought to invest his life and in the negotiations that followed. Correspondence with the London Missionary Society revealed that in order to go to China it would be necessary to receive training at Mansfield College, Oxford. But scholarships were not available. Bursaries were very limited. He could expect no financial help from home. It was as if God said through circumstances, "You were right in offering your life, but China is not the place."

Said the Home Missionary Society in Edinburgh, "Since the door to the foreign mission field seems closed, why not consider home missions?"

So Peter started going into Glasgow to Skerry's College three nights a week. He did not "get on" too well . . . Fulltime Christian work of any kind looked hopeless, impossibly far away.

At this juncture, James Broadbent, a cousin who had emigrated to the United States, came back to Scotland on a visit. . . .

Jim was busy looking at Peter's books when he came back.

"I don't understand this, Peter," he said. "What on earth is an engineer doing with *these* books—beginning Greek, Hebrew—of all things, all this theology and stuff?"

Peter flushed slightly. "Well, you see—Jim, I want to be a minister. It's rough going, though."

With a little encouragement from Jim, the whole story poured out—all of the developments, difficulties, and disappointments of the last years.

Jim looked very thoughtful. "You know, my early life was remarkably like yours. My father died when I was very young, just as your father, my Uncle Peter, did. I too had a

stepfather. I too had to fetch for myself. I was awfu' fond of
Uncle Peter. I'd do almost anything for his son. Look, Peter,
why don't you go to America to enter the ministry?"

"But Jim, I don't want to go to America. *Why should !?*
Besides, I haven't any money for passage."

. . . Peter prayed about it for three weeks, but no answer
came. Then one Sunday afternoon, as he was walking
through the rhododendron-lined lane in the Sholto Douglas
Estate, suddenly "the Chief" gave him his marching orders.

"It would be hard to describe to anyone how God can
make His will so plain to a man at times," Peter said later.
"I was walking along puzzling over the decision before me,
weighing this factor against that, as one does at such a time,
when all at once, *I knew*. The answer was just a clear-cut
strong inner conviction, quite unmistakable, that God wanted
me in the United States of America."

Now that the next step was plain, one might think that
difficulties and obstacles would melt away. Such was not the
case. The United States had stringent imigration laws. The
quota allotment each year from the British Isles was very
small. It took a year and a half to get a visa.

When finally Peter could sail, his cousin Jim was in Poland
on business. All alone he boarded the *Cameronia*. All alone
he watched the hills of Scotland sink into the cold waters
of the North Atlantic. He felt lonely and frightened.

Let Peter tell it in his own words in the sermon "Under
Sealed Orders" which he wrote in 1933:

I do not know what picture the phrase "Under Sealed
Orders" suggests to you.

In these terrible days, it may have several connota-
tions. . . .

To me, it recalls very vividly a scene from the First
World War, when I was a little boy, spending vacations
at a Scottish seaport.

I saw a gray destroyer slipping hurriedly from port in response to urgent orders . . .

I watched the crew hurry their preparations for sailing,
    watched them cast off the mooring hawsers . . .

Saw the sleek ship get under way, as she rose to meet the lazy ground swell of a summer evening . . .

    with her Morse lamp winking on the control bridge aft . . . Watched her until she was lost in the mists of the North Sea.

She was a mystery vessel.

She had sailed "under sealed orders."

I know something of what it means to go out like that for I have experienced it in my own life.

Well do I remember on the 19th of March, 1927, standing on the aft deck of the *Cameronia*,

    watching, with strangely moist eyes, the purple hills of the Mull of Kintyre sinking beneath the screw-thrashed waters of the Atlantic,

when every turn of the propeller was driving me farther from the land of my birth—from all I knew and loved.

And then—I walked slowly and wonderingly for'ard until I was leaning over the prow.

I stood looking into the west,

    wondering what lay behind that tumbling horizon—

    wondering what that unknown tomorrow held for me.

I, too, was going out in faith, "not knowing whither I went."

I was leaving the machine shops, where I had been working in a tube mill.

I was coming to the United States to enter the ministry, because I believed, with all my heart, that those were my orders from my Chief.

But I did not know how
    or when
    or where.

I could not foresee the wonderful way in which God
would open doors of opportunity.

I could never have imagined the romantic, thrilling way
in which God was to arrange my life . . .

   order my ways

      guide my steps

         provide for all my needs

           give me wonderful friends, generous helpers
until, at last, I would achieve His plan for me, and be
ordained a minister in the Gospel. . . .[3]

FLORENCE NIGHTINGALE

At this moment, in the midst of bustle, plans, discussions,
Florence received what she believed to be a call from God.

It is possible to know a great deal about Miss Nightingale's inner life because she had a habit of writing what she
called "private notes." She was unhappy in her environment,
she had no one to confide in, and she poured herself out
on paper. . . . In her private notes, written from girlhood to
old age, she recorded her true feelings.

It was in one of these that she wrote: "On February 7th,
1837, God spoke to me and called me to His service." She
heard, as Joan of Arc had, a voice outside herself, speaking
to her in human words.

She was not quite seventeen and her dream world was
often more actual to her than the real world. But the voices
which spoke to her were not a phenomenon of adolescence.
Nearly forty years later she wrote in a private note that her
"voices" had spoken to her four times. Once on February
7, 1837, the date of her call; once in 1853 before going to
her first post at the Hospital for Poor Gentlewomen in

3. From *A Man Called Peter* by Catherine Marshall. Copyright
1951 by Catherine Marshall. Used with permission of McGraw-
Hill Book Co.

Harley Street; once before the Crimea in 1854; and once after the death in 1861 of Sidney Herbert, her most influential friend and protector.

Her path was not made clear. God had called her, but what form that service was to take she did not know. The idea of nursing did not enter her mind. She doctored sick pets; she was especially fond of babies. Her protective instincts were strong, but they had not yet led her to the knowledge that God had called her to the service of the sick. Meanwhile she was at peace, full of confidence and faith. God had spoken to her once; presently He would speak to her again. . . .

In April the family left Paris, as Fanny [her mother] wished to spend the season in London and have the girls presented at Court. Fanny was well satisified. The tour had shown her that in Florence she possessed a daughter who promised to be exceptional. Florence's success in the intellectual world of Paris pleased her as much as her success at balls. She was graceful, witty, vividly good-looking. Her hair was of unusual beauty, thick, glossy and wavy. Fanny's pride in Florence was immense, her hopes for her brilliant.

They were doomed. Florence's conscience was awake, and the brief halcyon period was over. It was two years since God had spoken to her. Why had He not spoken again? The answer was evident—she was not worthy. She had forgotten God in the pleasure of balls and operas, in the vanity of being admired. In March, 1839, before she left Paris, she wrote in a private note that, to make herself worthy to be God's servant, the first temptation to be overcome was "the desire to shine in society."

. . . With the return of the Nightingales to London the first great struggle of Miss Nightingale's life began. It was divided into two stages and lasted fourteen years. First she groped within herself for five years before she reached the certainty that her "call" was to nurse the sick; next a bitter conflict with her family followed, and nine more years passed before she was able to nurse. . . .

The girls were caught up in a whirl of gaiety. Once more her "call" vanished from Florence's mind; she became absorbed in dresses and balls. She was deliriously happy, perpetually excited, and had been seized by a "passion" for her cousin Marianne Nicholson. . . . She was furiously discontented with herself; towards justifying her "call" she had done nothing. . . . But beneath the gay surface were agony and despair. It was three years since she had been "called" and she still did not know to what. How was she to make herself worthy so God could give her instructions? . . .

She worked at mathematics in her bedroom, and rose in the small hours to read philosophy and study Greek. She was discontented with life, even more discontented with herself. She blamed herself for her bad temper at home, for her unworthiness before God, as still she did not know what God had called her to do. . . .

"All I do is done to win admiration," she wrote in a private note. She cared too much, she went on, for "the pride of life."

England in 1842 was in the grip of what has passed into history as "the hungry forties." Everywhere were starvation, sweated labor, and dirt. Diseased scarecrows swarmed not only in the airless undrained courts of London but in the "black filth" of rural cottages; workhouses, hospitals, and prisons were overflowing. Florence wrote in a private note: "My mind is absorbed with the idea of the sufferings of man. . . . All the people I see are eaten up with care or poverty or disease."

She knew now that her destiny lay among the miserable, outside her little world of ease and comfort. But what form it was to take, she still had no idea. . . .

Yet she was approaching a secret decision of the utmost importance and some time in the following spring the knowledge came to her that her vocation lay in hospitals among the sick. At last, seven years after her "call" her destiny was clear. "Since I was twenty-four," she wrote later," . . . there never was any vagueness in my plans or ideas as to what God's work was for me."

In June Dr. Samuel Gridley Howe, the American philanthropist, came to Embley. On the night of his arrival Florence spoke to him privately: "Dr. Howe, do you think it would be unsuitable and unbecoming for a young Englishwoman to devote herself to works of charity in hospitals and elsewhere as Catholic sisters do?" He gave a sincere answer: "My dear Miss Florence, it would be unusual, and in England whatever is unusual is thought to be unsuitable; but I say to you 'go forward,' if you have a vocation for that way of life, act up to your inspiration and you will find there is never anything unbecoming or unladylike in doing your duty for the good of others. Choose, go on with it, wherever it may lead you, and God be with you."

. . . Life in this setting was what Florence Nightingale was now considering. But a year passed and she became more wretchedly unhappy; in vain she had dug after a plan which could conceivably result in her going to work in hospitals. Eight years had passed since her "call," and not merely had she accomplished nothing, she had slipped backwards—she had lost the sense of walking with God. She reproached herself bitterly. . . .

One of the extradordinary features of Miss Nightingale's life is the passage of time. She starts with a "call" in 1837. Seven years pass before she finds out what she has been called to do. Nine more years pass before she gains freedom in 1853 to pursue her vocation. Sixteen years in all, during which the eager susceptible girl was slowly hammered into the steely powerful woman of genius. The last eight years, after her failure in 1845, were years in which suffering piled on suffering, frustration followed frustration, until she was brought to the verge of madness.

The bonds which bound her were only of straw, but she

did not break them. She could act only when she felt moral justification, and she felt no moral justification. She spent sleepless nights, wrestling with her soul, seeking with tears and prayers to make herself worthy to receive the kindness of God. And dreaming enslaved her more and more as she carried out the duties of a daughter. Many of her dreams centered upon Richard Monckton Milnes. She imagined herself married to him, performing heroic deeds with him. . . .

So month followed month—it seemed uneventfully, but in her character a profound change was taking place. "I feel," she wrote in 1846, "as if all my being were gradually drawing together to one point." She decided that her longing for affection was too powerful for safety, and she began deliberately to detach herself from human relationships. Love, marriage, even friendship, must be renounced. But she could not bring herself yet to face losing Richard Monckton Milnes. The desire to be loved died hard. . . .

She succumbed to dreaming, helplessly, shamefully. She dreamed of fame, of Richard Monckton Milnes. To escape from dreaming she sought relief in nursing the poor of the village of Wellow. Fanny and Parthe became irritated: it was unnecessary for Florence to go into the "black filth" of the cottages, actually touching sick people and even making their beds; she would bring an infectious disease into the house and kill her sister. She visited her sick in secret, runnig back breathless through the muddy lanes to be in time for dinner. W.E.N., who hated dirt, disease and ugliness, was disgusted. He told Florence she was being theatrical; if she wanted something to do, let her work in the village school. She did for a time, but she failed. "I was disgusted with my utter impotence," she wrote. "I made no improvement. . . . Why should I? . . . Education I know is not my genius."

In March, when the Nightingales went to London for the season, Florence was in a mounting delirium of self-reproach and frustration. Dreaming became uncontrollable. She was convinced that she was going insane. In this wretched state another blow fell. Richard Monckton Milnes, after seven years, would be put off no longer. He insisted on a definite answer—would she marry him or not? She refused.

It was an act which required extraordinary courage. She was deeply stirred by him, she called him "the man I adored"; and she renounced him for the sake of a destiny which it seemed impossible she would ever fulfill. . . .

Two figures emerged from the Crimea as heroic, the soldier and the nurse. In each case a transformation in public estimation took place, and in each case the transformation was due to Miss Nightingale. Never again was the British soldier to be ranked as the scum of the earth, nor the nurse pictured as a tipsy, promiscuous harridan. Miss Nightingale had stamped the profession of nurse with her own image. She ended the Crimean War obsessed by a sense of failure. Yet, in the midst of the muddle and the filth, the agony and the defeats, she had brought about a revolution.[4]

ALAN REDPATH

I came to know Christ as my Saviour when I was almost twenty years of age through the ministry of a colleague in the office in which I was working while training to be a chartered accountant. His life was so consistent and so Christlike—revealing that it was impossible in his presence to be neutral about the Lord. Following my conversion I went with my friend to Brethren meetings every week (you see, I had a good beginning!).

For several months I attended a weekly Bible Study meeting at a Brethren Hall in the north of England, where I became increasingly convinced that the Christian Life involved

4. From *Florence Nightingale* by Cecil Woodham-Smith. As condensed in the August 1951 *Reader's Digest*. Copyright 1951 by Cecil Woodham-Smith. Used with permission of McGraw-Hill Book Co.

discipleship and meant different standards altogether from the life which I had previously lived. I faced the words of the Saviour when He said, "If any man will come after me, let him deny himself, take up his cross, and follow me"; but on the other hand I faced the appeal of all the attractive alternatives which seemed so real to me at the time, and I am ashamed to say that for several years the latter won the day. I had no place in my life for the Cross, no place for witness or testimony. I knew I was a Christian because, while trying hard to find my amusement in the world, I was so miserable! Before I was converted these things had filled my life with pleasure, but now I instinctively knew that I was out of God's will. I remember the friend who led me to the Lord coming down to London and having lunch with me one day when I was on the staff of I.C.I. as a chartered accountant, and he said to me, *"You know, it is possible to have a saved soul but a wasted life."* Those words stabbed me awake, and though I continued for some time in my rebellion, I grew more and more miserable until eventually the Lord broke me down, and my life was given completely to Him.

Soon afterwards I came in touch with the National Young Life Campaign and the Brothers Wood. Under their guidance I attended a School of Evangelism that was held in the mid-thirties in London, and it was there that I began to feel the tremendous appeal to preach the Gospel. There were opportunities given me to take part in Youth Witness Teams, and so the fire began to burn, and my heart began to be deeply stirred with the need of the unsaved. By that time I was married, and my wife and I were involved in Christian work and witness, which became increasingly dear to us, and which presented an increasing challenge.

At the same time responsibilities in business were growing, and somehow I sensed that, for me at least, the two were in conflict. My wife and I faced this issue on our knees before the Lord, and I remember to this day taking out a piece of paper, drawing a line down the middle, and on one side putting "Arguments in favour of staying in business," and on the other side "Arguments in favour of going into the ministry." There were about an equal number on each side of the line at first. Arguments in favor of staying in business were the opportunity of witness to business colleagues, and entry into a circle of life which I would not perhaps reach in the ministry; also a sense of obligation to my parents who had sacrificed everything in order to enable me to have a business training. On the other hand, on the other side of the line, there were opportunities for preaching, more time for Bible study and prayer (I have long since crossed that one out, because it just isn't true: even in the ministry such time has to be made); the giving of my whole time to the Lord and His work.

It was some thirteen months later, in response to the daily reading of the Word and in prayer, that the Lord made it abundantly clear to me that the arguments in favour of staying in business did not carry any conviction and, therefore, it was with a fearful and trembling heart, and yet with a deep conviction of the Spirit that I was in the will of God, that I handed in my resignation and joined the staff of the National Young Life Campaign in 1936.

I had no opportunity for theological training, as it was impossible for me to start then and at the same time maintain my home. I remember going to see Dr. Graham Scroggie, who had been a great help to me, and asking him for a list of fifty books which he would recommend to a young man with business training but no theological background, who had a great burden in his heart to preach the Gospel and enter the ministry. He gave me the list of books, many of them his own publications for which I have been eternally grateful, and as I went into evangelism I gave myself to the study of the Word and prayer, and it was in the context of evangelistic ministry for four years, travelling up and down the country, that I studied and prayed and enjoyed the thrill of the blessing of God in my own heart.

I look back over thirty years of ministry, and have been deeply conscious of the Lord's grace and strength all through my life. I have never doubted my call, though sometimes the battles and conflicts have been tremendous . . .

Preaching, however, has always been my greatest joy, and in recent years the Lord has seen fit to put me through a deep experience of chastening through illness, which has more firmly than ever established this as the priority of my life. . . . There is no task like it this side of heaven. May the Lord call a great company into the ministry of His word in these momentous days. The need is desperate for it is still true, to our shame, that while the harvest still is plenteous, the labourers are so tragically few. If, however, you can find reason for not going into the ministry, then by all means stay out of it, for only the man who is in it by divine compulsion and knows that he could not be happy anywhere else will be able to stand the tests that are sure to come. In any case, whether in the "full-time" ministry or not, the concern of us all who know Christ as Lord should be "Woe is me if I preach not the gospel." [5]

TOM SKINNER

The streets of Harlem are always crowded. Except when the weather is really bad, there are sometimes hundreds of people just standing on the corners.

There is the derelict, without work, without money, without hope of ever having dignity.

There are the thousands of drug addicts—some 60,000 in Harlem—pacing nervously while waiting for a "pusher"

5. Alan Redpath: *My Call to Preach,* edited by C. A. Joyce. London: Marshall, Morgan & Scott, 1968, pp. 105-110. Used by permission.

to come by to give them another "fix." Some of the addicts are looking for things to steal to pay for their next shot.

Prostitutes try to "hustle" customers to pay for their drugs —or the drugs of husbands.

And when school is out, the kids are on the streets. They roam from early morning until sometimes after midnight. The eight-to-ten-year olds are forming sub-gangs.

After my conversion, these people became my concern. I became deeply concerned about thousands of other fellows like Tom Skinner who needed to hear the truth about this person Jesus Christ. They needed someone on their own level, someone who understood their language, someone who understood the anguish, suffering, and frustration that develop when a kid is born and raised in a community like Harlem. I know the bitterness of the kid who feels trapped —who feels there is no opportunity, no way out for him. If he can hear the truth about Jesus Christ, it can be the most liberating force in his life. For the first time he can pick up his head and really begin to live.

Jesus Christ says, "I have come that they might have life, and that they might have it more abundantly."

This is the message for the people of the street, for Harlem. We didn't have to go search for them, we didn't have to look for them, we didn't have to have anything to attract them. They were there. It was just a matter of knowing how to communicate and to get the word to them that Jesus Christ cared—about them.

Following my conversion, I led several of my former gang to the Lord. I was thrilled to see my faith reproduce itself through the Holy Spirit working in the lives of the guys. But I prayed for more effective ways of reaching the thousands of kids in Harlem.

Without giving much thought to the serious implications involved, a group of us picked out certain days during the week and went out in the street to confront individuals with the claims of Jesus Christ. Sometimes we would rent portable loudspeakers and stand on the street corner and actually have large street meetings. This wasn't too difficult when you consider the fact that as many as six hundred people are within earshot on a street corner, and sometimes maybe even a thousand. You can get a good listening audience with the many hundreds of people going back and forth.

One of my first experiences was an effort that took us down to 118th Street, around Fifth Avenue. It's a heavily populated area—an area where the gang known as the "Diablos" operated. . . . And there on the street corner, we led at least twenty-five members of the Diablo gang to Jesus Christ. Many of them prayed openly on the street. And for a person who had just come to know Jesus Christ only a few weeks, for a person who was just now beginning to enter into a phase of witnessing about Jesus Christ to other people, this was a most thrilling moment.

We began to see results like this in many different communities and on many street corners. Day after day, we made it our business to attempt to win at least one person to Jesus Christ, to witness of the saving power and ability of this Person, Jesus Christ. And we saw fellows who were the potential top racketeers in New York City finding Jesus Christ. We saw girls who, if they were allowed to go the way they were traveling, would end up as prostitutes or drug addicts. Some of them, if they continued, would end up raising five or six children on welfare without a father. But now, because we had the opportunity of meeting them when they were in their early teens, and confronting them with the claims of Jesus Christ, their lives were being redirected.

On the weekends, we dressed up in dungarees, polo shirts, and dirty sneakers, and picked out a target community. We went to the basketball courts in the communities where we knew a known gang was operating. There we would play on that basketball court day after day, four or five hours a day, until we got to know the leader of the guys in the neighborhood. Once we found him, we tried to win him as a friend—not to try and cram religion down his throat. You see, so many of these fellows on the street can't believe anyone really cares about them. Even in the gang it's difficult for a guy to trust someone as a friend. Most guys who belong to gangs live in constant fear, wondering who is going to turn against them, who is going to try to challenge their leadership, who is going to try to outdo them.

But once we won this fellow as a friend, we began the process of sharing with him what Jesus Christ had done in our own personal lives. And what a thrill it was to see one guy after another, one gang leader after another, one gang member after another, turning to Jesus Christ. We became tremendously excited about this ministry that God had committed to us. This business of witnessing to guys and girls at school, on street corners, in basement hideouts, recreation centers, and playgrounds went on quietly.

During this time, I was also enrolled in Bible school classes at the Manhattan Bible Institute in New York City. There I was being rounded in the fundamentals of theology and Scripture.

Balancing my ministry to the street gangs was a ministry to kids in church. These teenagers were in church and only going through the motions, just as I had been doing before I came to know Christ. Many of them found it difficult to understand what it meant to know—in an experience of faith—Jesus Christ. Often, I found myself coming into open conflict with some of the leading pastors within the association of Negro churches (men who were not teaching their young people about the claims of Jesus Christ).

Many of the young people, though, became very interested and invited me to their churches to discuss these issues with them. I went eagerly—and tried to challenge these young people about what it means to really know Christ, what it means to have Christ living in an individual. I told them how Christ could make it possible for us to live upright lives before God. The tragedy was that I was too late for many of these young people. At sixteen or seventeen, they were already well experienced in premarital sex, narcotics, and crime. Many of the girls in these churches were dropping out of high school and subsequently church because they were pregnant. Many of them were becoming disgusted with church because of the extramarital affairs that were going on between ministers, deacons, and other leaders of the churches. These young people knew what was happening and they were looking for something real. And they weren't finding it in church.

As I began to get into their churches and speak in their youth department meetings, I began to see results. I saw teenagers responding to the claims of Jesus Christ.

Some pastors were beginning to see some real results among the young people. They invited me to conduct week-long meetings in their churches among the young people.

That is the way my preaching ministry began. And we really saw God begin to work.[6]

PAUL S. REES

When asked to give an account of my "call" to the ministry, I am obliged to disappoint any who expect a vivid description of some single mighty moment, some dramatic episode of overpowering impact that suddenly settled it: "This is my calling!" Recalling the phrases of Frederick Atkinson's lively hymn, "Spirit of God, descend upon my heart," I should have to say that my sense of vocation was neither signified nor sealed by "prophetic ecstasies" or "sudden rending of the veil of clay," or "angel visit," or "opening skies." On the contrary, the mold into which God was pleased to pour my summons to the pulpit might be described in language that John Newton once used in

6. From *Black and Free* by Tom Skinner. Copyright © 1968 by Zondervan Publishing House and used by permission.

writing to a friend about the ministerial vocation: "a gradual train of circumstances pointing out the means, the time, the place, of actually entering upon the work."

The call of God to me suggests, first of all, *a combination of predisposing influences*. For example, there was the home climate of my childhood. It was a Quaker family in which I was nurtured. Among the progressive "Friends" (as distinguished from those who clung more strictly to silent meetings) my father found acceptance both as pastor and evangelist. And, since the Quakers were prepared to recognize the ministerial calling of women, my mother was a "recorded" preacher. Not since I learned to read can I recall a time in my boyhood when I did not frequently come on the sermon notes and manuscripts belonging either to my father or my mother.

It would be wrong, however, if I left the impression that my parents tried to "steer" me into the ministry, that they put pressure on me to step forward and offer for the preaching task. Indeed (and here my memory may not be wholly reliable) I was not given the feeling that if I failed to enter the ministry, they would be disappointed. That they would have been disappointed is, I think, beyond question. The point is that they tried not to make me feel that they would. This was in keeping with my father's conviction that no man should be in the ministry if he could stay out of it!

Outside the family, moreover, there were the expectations of others which, to some degree, must have predisposed me in favor of the ministerial vocation. This influence, admittedly, was often casual, as when someone would say, as though for lack of anything else to communicate, "I suppose you are going to be a preacher like your father." At other times the impact was thoughtful, as in the case of an elderly, scholarly friend of my father's who was leading us in our family prayers. Moving on his knees to where I was kneeling, he put his hands on my head and prayed, "Lord, lay your hand on Paul; make him a preacher of the gospel; fill him with the Holy Ghost; and send him around the world like a flame of fire."

. . . There is a second consideration I should have to take into account in any attempt to reconstruct my "call to preach." It is something I might describe as the *commingling of issues*. In most instances it is a man already "in Christ" who is confronted by this vocational question: Does God want me in the ministry? In my case it was different. I was seventeen. Culturally and sentimentally, I was a Christian. In the deepest sense I was not! I was the "elder brother" who had never openly and flagrantly rebelled against the rule of the house. I knew nothing of the hogs and harlots that symbolized the degradation of the prodigal. I was the Pharisee who needed to see and feel sin in a dimension that the self-righteous find it terribly hard to grasp. Child of the parsonage? Yes. But also, child of Satan! Instructed in the "way of salvation"? Yes. Instructed, but not inducted! . . .

Something else belongs to my story. I shall call it the *climax of surrender*. For many years my father had been a far more than average student of the literature of Christian sanctity. He was something of a mystic himself, though never an ascetic, never an impractical visionary. As a Quaker he had drunk freely from the fountains opened by George Fox, William Barclay, John Woolman, and others. Far beyond this, he had ranged through the writings of the German pietists, the French saints, and the extensive publications of John Wesley, John Fletcher, Adam Clarke, and the early Methodists. The Holy Spirit and, through His power, the offered life of Christian wholeness, or holiness, were acutely real to my father. I had absorbed from his example and preaching a kind of theological framework in which the *conscious* realization of Christ's lordship over all of life came to the Christian as something distinguishable from his conversion. (Fifty years later I am persuaded that this is typically, though not necessarily, true.)

In any case, something occurred only days after my peace-with-God exeprience. I had been alone in my room. My spirit was gay. I am afraid there is no other way to be truthful about it. I was a different person. Of this there could be no doubt. Yet there was this awareness of some "unfinished business" that I had with God. The unsettled question of my vocation! The unappropriated promise, "You shall receive power when the Holy Spirit has come upon you!"

Thirty-five years later I was to hear Dr. John Sutherland Bonnell of New York's Fifth Avenue Presbyterian Church tell me of a conversation he had with a mature psychiatrist. Bonnell asked him if he could give in a word or a phrase the one thing that unlocked more doors to mental and emotional health than any other. The seasoned counsellor replied: "The word 'surrender.' "

This I know: while walking along the hall of our California bungalow, following a period of quiet meditation in my room, the Inner Voice said, "Why not *now*?" I unresistingly answered, "Yes, Lord, *now!*" Was it blind surrender? I think not. It included my commitment to be a preacher, but it went deeper. In memory and gratitude I have relived that moment times without number. It is, I suppose, next to impossible to prevent the maturing experience of the years from coloring and distorting the bare facts of such a personal event in the life of a seventeen-year-old. To the best of my recollection, what stood out in my mind above everything else was (1) Christ as Lord, (2) the Holy Spirit as power, (3) myself as not my own, surrendered, crucified. There was an incredible calmness and clarity about the whole affair. . . .

I write these intimately personal lines within weeks of the time that I shall gratefully celebrate the golden anniversary of that first callow attempt at preaching. The long years in between have meant "trial and error," learning and unlearning, the deep satisfactions that arise from shepherding the same flock for twenty years and the exhilarating rewards of roaming the world as an evangelist and Bible teacher. On some points my mind has been open enough to be changed, flexible enough (I trust) to adapt, sensitive enough to respond to new ranges of stimuli, but on one point (among others) it has been neither changed nor seriously challenged: my call to preach was *God's* commission entrusted to me.

My mother was Swedish, not Scottish. Had she been the latter, she might well have said to me, in the language of the lovely mother in *Beside the Bonnie Brier Bush* to her laddie facing the ministry:

> Ye'll follow Christ, and gin He offers you His cross, ye'll no refuse it, for He aye carries the heavy end Himself.

He does indeed!

The thousand proofs of it, so mercifully given me, fill me with praise.[7]

7. Paul S. Rees: *My Call to Preach*, edited by C. A. Joyce. London: Marshall, Morgan & Scott, 1968, pp. 111-118. Used by permission.

16

THE ULTIMATE CALL
OR THE HOPE
OF HIS CALLING

The title of this chapter is based not on the reference to a last or final call but primarily the concept of the "highest" call, qualitatively speaking.

In affinity with what has been stressed in previous chapters, this *ultimate call* of God to service is intertwined with the *ultimate will* of God. Since the call of God at the outset is the same as the will of God, so the ultimate of both the call and the will is reached only to the extent they remain wedded in continuous union.

To fully comprehend what is meant by the ultimate call of God to service, it is necessary to understand what is meant by "the ultimate will of God."

. . . It is very basic that we recognize and constantly bear in mind that there are three phases to this area of the will of God:

God's *active* will
God's *permissive* will
God's *ultimate* will

. . . In doing this, it is most important to keep in mind that the exclusive isolation of each of these phases is totally impossible. In fact, they are so interrelated and intertwined that it is not only impossible to dissect them into separate components but also impossible to distinguish where the one begins and the other ends. . . . God's plan and purpose for our life as an individual is never an island by itself. It is part and parcel of His plan for and related to His total plan for all of mankind, which eventuates in glory for Himself. Make no mistake about it, the will of God for us is inherent in the glory of God. Therefore, when man cooperates unreservedly with God, with an absolute dedication to Him, God's will, the purpose and plan, is accomplished in and through the life of His saint! . . .

By this positive set of declarations God ensures He will ultimately bring into being His plan and program for that individual who has sought to live for His honor and glory. What God wills He not only can, but does perform, our will is in harmony with His. This is axiomatic! . . .

Possibly some readers are still asking the question, "Just what is the ultimate will of God?" While the answer is not simple, it could be defined as, "God's plan or program to recreate man in His own image and thereby reveal His own glory through the life and service of the individual." . . .

This definition may be amplified as that part of God's active or perfect will that is achieved after and in spite of hindrances and obstacles by evil and other exterior forces not under the control of God. This always leads into that service to God which is *most glorifying* to Him and most satisfying to His servant. What form of service this may take is not always apparent. No matter! What is most important is the absolute submission to God's will.[1]
Paul refers to this ultimate call in the term "the *hope* of

1 Deratany Edward: *Refuge in the Secret Place.* Glendale, Calif.: Regal Books, 1971, pp. 117, 118, 146, 152, 153.

His Calling." His earnest desire for the saints to comprehend and attain this is expressed in the context:

> (For I always pray) the God of our Lord Jesus Christ,
> the Father of Glory, that He may grant you a spirit of
> wisdom and revelation—of insight into mysteries and
> secrets—in the (deep and intimate) knowledge of Him,
> By having the eyes of your heart flooded with light, so
> that you can know and understand the hope to which He
> has called and how rich is His glorious inheritance in the
> saints—His set-apart ones (Eph. 1:17, 18) (AB).

The first thing to remember is that God *initiates* this calling. No human being can call himself to God's image and service. God is the prime moving factor in any call.

Secondly, this "hope" is for "the called ones," "His set-apart ones." Admittedly, this includes *all* who are called, whether to salvation, sanctification, or service and whether to general or special service. For our purposes, we take the liberty of referring this "hope" particularly to the call to service, and more specifically, to special service.

Thirdly, this so-called hope is the ultimate to which "the called of God" aspire. It is their goal, their ambition, and the motivating factor, energized by love for God, which seal their consecration and dedication to fulfill His call and will.

SUFFERING

This hope may be described and summarized in two words: *suffering* and *glory*. The idea of suffering may not initially seem to have substantive relationship to any kind of a hope, nor does this appear to be an eagerly sought or hoped-for experience. On closer examination of the total context of Scripture, the outworking of God's will makes this first phase of His calling (this call to *share* Christ's suffering) a privilege exceedingly beneficial. To the extent that we *share this suffering*—we shall *share His glory*.

The Spirit Himself (thus) testifies together with our own spirit, (assuring us) that we are children of God.

And if we are (His) children then we are (His) heirs also: heirs of God and *fellow heirs* with Christ—sharing His inheritance with Him; only we must share His suffering if we are to share His Glory.

(But what of that?) For I consider that the sufferings of this present time (this present life) are not worth being compared with the glory that is about to be revealed to us and in us and for us, and conferred on us! (Rom. 8:16–18) (AB).

The great apostle, Peter, shows the maturity of his experience as against his earlier defeats when speaking of this call to share Christ's suffering.

For even to this were you called—it is inseparable from your vocation. For Christ also suffered for you, leaving you (His personal) example, so that you should follow on in His footsteps (1 Peter 2:21) (AB).

The New American Standard Bible interprets this verse, which is directed to the elect, that they (and we) are "called for this purpose" (i.e. suffering). After Peter has concluded his counseling of the elect, he summarily and climatically points out that this suffering rises to that other phase of the hope of His calling—glory.

And after you have suffered a little while, the God of all grace—Who imparts all blessing and favor—Who has called you to His (own) eternal glory in Christ Jesus, will Himself complete and make what you ought to be, establish and ground your securely, and strengthen (and settle) you (1 Peter 5:10) (AB).

GLORY

Although Peter is our prime resource for our understanding of this "call to suffering," we turn to Paul who gives us a comprehensive picture of the "call to glory." In his epistle to the Ephesians (1:18), he mentions his prayers for the saints, "the consecrated, set apart ones." The objective of his prayers, he declares, is that they might *know* "the hope of His calling." In the broader context of his prayer (found in Ephesians 1:16–19 AB) this hope includes:

1. "A spirit of wisdom." This is not merely an accumulation of knowledge and facts but rather an "insight into mysteries and secrets" reserved for the called ones.
2. A "deep and initimate knowledge of him." This contrasts with a superficial acquaintance of Christ.
3. An understanding of the richness of "His glorious inheritance in the saints—His set apart ones." Peter underscores this with "you are called for the very purpose that you might *inherit* a blessing" (Peter 3:9).
4. A knowledge and an understanding of "the immeasurable, unlimited and surpassing greatness of His power in and for us who believe, as demonstrated in the working of His mighty strength."

To sense more fully the impact of what Paul is describing and the value of what it is to share His glory, we need to catch a vision of what that glory is. The glory of anything is its highest qualities or attributes. On occasion, such as when Moses was with God on Mount Sinai and requested, "Show me thy glory" (Exod. 33:18), we may catch a glimpse of Christ's glory. At best, we can only *partially* view or apprehend His glory, in this life. And even the partial sharing of this present glory is reserved only for the called ones (initially to salvation, continuously to godliness and service, and eventually to full glory):

But, on the contrary, as the Scripture says, What eye

has not seen, and ear has not heard, and has not entered into the heart of man, (all that) God has prepared—made and keeps ready—for those who love Him (that is, for those who hold Him in affectionate reverence, promptly obeying Him and gratefully recognizing the benefits He has bestowed) (Isa. 64:4; 65:17).

Yet to us God has unveiled and revealed them by and through His Spirit, for the (Holy) Spirit searches diligently, exploring and examining everything, even sounding the profound and bottomless things of God—the divine counsels and things hidden and beyond man's scrutiny (1 Cor. 2:9, 10) (AB).

GRACE

Man, in his highest achievements, can never attain to the glory of Christ in this life. Yet, in the outworking of His love and mercy, God graciously allows us to *share* in this glory, partially now but ultimately later. This is all-inclusive in the Call of God. (Continue to bear in mind, the call to salvation and sanctification always involves service.) The Bible is full of this truth:

And it was for this *He called you* through our gospel, *that you may gain the glory of our Lord Jesus Christ* (2 Thess. 2:15) (NASB).

. . . walk in a manner worthy of the God who *calls you into His* own kingdom and *glory* (1 Thess. 2:12) (NASB).

And all of us, as with unveiled face, (because we) continued to behold (in the Word of God) as in a mirror the glory of the Lord, are constantly being transfigured into His very own image in ever increasing splendor and from one degree of glory to another; (for this comes) from the Lord (Who is) the Spirit (2 Cor. 3:18) (AB).*

---

* Italics added.

Our only hope and claim to this glorious privilege results from the favor and sovereignty of God. It is almost repugnant to witness the evidence of pride in some individuals who struggle over the call of God, this invitation to share in His glory. In a shallow, reluctant dedication they appear to surrender with the attitude, "O.K. God, I'll do what You want me to do—but it's at a personal sacrifice. I'm really not anxious or wholeheartedly willing to do this—but if it's what you want, I'll go. In reality, I'm doing You a favor by this surrender." This type of dedication precludes the sharing of His glory. Only to the extent there is a sincere recognition of our unworthiness and His grace, accomplished by a wholehearted, humble obedience to His call, can we experience the sharing of this ultimate glory. Then by His grace and His grace alone are we counted worthy or "made worthy" of our calling.

> When He comes to be glorified in His saints on that day, and to be marveled at among all who have believed —for our testimony to you was believed. To this end also we *pray* for you always that our *God may count you worthy of your calling,* and fulfill every desire for goodness and the work of faith with power;
>
> In order that the name of our Lord Jesus may be glorified in you, and you in Him, according to the grace of our God and the Lord Jesus Christ (2 Thess: 1:10–12) (NASB).*

In the context of the first chapter of his second epistle, Peter lists certain desirable qualities pertaining to godliness achieved "through the knowledge of Him who called us to glory and virtue." He goes on to show that to lack these is to be spiritually blind or shortsighted. In contrast, the possession and development of these will make void any idleness or unfruitfulness.

* Italics added.

For as these qualities are yours and increasingly abound in you, they will keep (you) from being idle or unfruitful into the (full personal) knowledge of our Lord Jesus Christ, the Messiah, the Anointed One (2 Peter 1:8) (AB).

To underscore the importance of the positive aspect, industry and fruitfulness, he admonishes his readers:

Because of this, brethren, be all the more solicitious and eager to make sure (to ratify, to strengthen, to make steadfast) your calling and election; for if you do this you will never stumble or fall (2 Peter 1:10) (AB).

Admittedly, again, all this is in reference to holiness and godliness. But, based on our initial premise, inherent in this ultimate call to living is the ultimate call to service.

The final word of divine revelation on this total subject comes to us from the pen of the Apostle Paul:

Therefore, my beloved brethren, be firm (steadfast), immovable, always abounding in the work of the Lord— that is, always being *superior* (excelling, doing more than enough) in the service of the Lord, and knowing and being continually aware that your labor in the Lord is not futile—never wasted or to no purpose. (1 Cor. 15:58) (AB).